NO DAYS OFF

My Life with Type 1 Diabetes
and Journey to the NHL

MAX DOMI

with

Jim Lang

Published by Simon & Schuster

NEW YORK LONDON TORONTO SYDNEY NEW DELHI

SIMON &
SCHUSTER
CANADA

A Division of Simon & Schuster, Inc.
166 King Street East, Suite 300
Toronto, Ontario, M5A 1J3

This Simon & Schuster Canada edition October 2019

SIMON & SCHUSTER CANADA and colophon are trademarks
of Simon & Schuster, Inc.

For information about special discounts for bulk purchases,
please contact Simon & Schuster Special Sales at 1-800-268-3216
or CustomerService@simonandschuster.ca.

Library and Archives Canada Cataloguing in Publication

Title: No days off : my life with type 1 diabetes and journey to the NHL/ Max Domi.
        Names: Domi, Max, 1995– author.
Identifiers: Canadiana (print) 20190092610 | Canadiana (ebook) 20190092629 |
        ISBN 9781501183645 (hardcover) | ISBN 9781982103408 (signed hardcover) |
        ISBN 9781501183652 (ebook)
Subjects: LCSH: Domi, Max, 1995- | LCSH: Domi, Max, 1995   —Health. |
        LCSH: Diabetics—Canada— Biography. | LCSH: Hockey players—Canada—
        Biography. | LCGFT: Autobiographies.
Classification: LCC RC660 .85 2019 | DDC 362.196/46220092—dc23

Manufactured in Canada

10   9   8   7   6   5   4   3   2   1

ISBN 978-1-5011-8364-5
ISBN 978-1-5011-8365-2 (ebook)

To every kid dealing with type 1 diabetes,
their friends and family, and anyone else
who wants to follow their dreams

CONTENTS

INTRODUCTION

The 2013 NHL Entry Draft was held on June 30. I'd been looking forward to that day ever since I'd first put on a pair of skates and told myself that one day I'd play in the NHL. I'd been working toward that dream for most of my life, and now the day had finally arrived when I would get to take the biggest step toward realizing it.

But the morning of the draft, all of my excitement from the previous weeks and months was gone. In its place was a bundle of nerves. Nervousness can definitely take its toll on your blood sugar levels—big swings in your emotional state in general can throw off your blood sugar, going low or high like that can then lead to more mood changes, and the spiral continues. It's only worse when you don't have enough to eat.

I knew that, but when I joined my dad at the breakfast table in our family friend's apartment that morning, I had no appetite. My dad watched me pick at my food for a while before he handed me a rice cake with peanut butter on it. "It doesn't matter how nervous you are, it's going to be a long day," he said. "You have to eat." My health came first.

We left the apartment and met up with my mom and sisters at their hotel. Just as we were about to leave for the arena, I felt a wave of exhaustion hit me. Then my vision started to get a little blurry. *Not now*, I thought.

"I'm going low," I said to my parents. My blood sugar had plummeted, and I needed to get it back up or else things would get worse.

My dad immediately went to buy some juice for me. I felt a little uneasy, so I sat down on the couch, where my mom kept watch over me. Luckily, with a bit of rest and some sugar back in my system, I managed to balance myself out, and we were able to make it onto the bus to the draft.

When we finally got to the arena, we settled into our seats in the fifth row, close to the stage. Nathan MacKinnon and Seth Jones were both sitting in front of us with their families. I leaned over to my parents and whispered, "Nate is going to go number one overall." Sure enough, a few minutes later, Nate's name was the first one announced, and the arena erupted in applause and cheers.

A few more picks went by, and I still didn't hear my name called. Suddenly, I felt the familiar sensation of going low wash over me. I realized I'd made a mistake. I'd been so caught up in the draft that I hadn't paid attention to the time that passed between each selection. It seemed to take forever for each team's representatives to walk to the stage, and then the players had a long walk to cross the floor whenever their name was called. My blood sugar had already dropped low at the hotel, and here, two hours later, I was low again.

At my feet I had a blue Gatorade and a couple of juices to help get my blood sugar up. I tried to be discreet, leaning over every once in a while to take a sip. I desperately needed it—my lack of breakfast that morning was catching up to me.

Every time a general manager approached the podium, my dad turned to me and said, "This is the one!" The first couple of times, I felt my pulse quicken when he said it, hoping he was right. But each time my name wasn't called, my excitement died down and my nervousness flared back up.

The lack of food and emotional swings were throwing my blood sugar completely off, and I was starting to get frustrated. Not at anyone or anything in particular, but just an irritability that I knew would go away if I got my blood sugar back where it needed to be. I tried to silence the negative voice in the back of my head and stay positive. *This is your moment*, I thought.

About half an hour into the event, Don Maloney, the Phoenix Coyotes' general manager, approached the podium for the twelfth pick of the day.

"The Phoenix Coyotes," Maloney said, "are proud to select, from the London Knights of the OHL, Max Domi."

I jumped out of my seat from sheer excitement as the Coyotes howl played throughout the arena. I was so happy that I didn't know which way to turn. My dad was still sitting down, and I couldn't understand why—I'd leapt up so quickly he hadn't had time to react. He got to his feet, and I gave him a hug, and then I turned to give my mom the same.

As I walked across the floor toward the stage, I felt like I was floating. I couldn't believe that my dreams were finally coming true. The excitement coursing through me, along with the applause from the crowd and the stage lights, was making my head spin. I took a deep breath as I felt the Bambi legs starting to creep back. When I got to the stairs to the stage, the only thing I could think was, *Don't trip.*

I couldn't hear it, but as I walked across the stage, shaking each of the Coyotes officials' hand and thanking them for drafting me, the TV broadcasters were talking about my diabetes. They even pointed out what they thought was my insulin pump on my belt. I did own an insulin pump, but I'd temporarily disconnected it, which I would do when my blood sugar got low and I needed to prevent any more insulin from entering my system. What the announcers thought was my insulin pump was actually just the microphone pack the event organizers had given me.

I might not have been wearing an insulin pump as I pulled on my very first NHL jersey, but I still carried my diabetes with me. It was baggage I was never able to put down; it was part of who I was.

Making the NHL had always been my dream, and being drafted that day was the greatest accomplishment of my life to that point. As my new reality sunk in, I reflected on what had brought me to that place and the journey that lay ahead. The more I thought about it, the more I realized that I hadn't made it that far despite my diabetes, but because of it.

My diabetes is my 24/7 constant companion. And like anyone who suffers from type 1 diabetes—or any other lifelong disease— I never get a day off. But as difficult as my diagnosis has made many things in my life, it's never stopped me from chasing my dream. Every day brings with it a new test and a new opportunity. And lucky for me, I've always liked a challenge.

NO DAYS OFF

1

FAMILY FIRST

I was just five weeks old when I experienced my first NHL trade.

Technically, it wasn't *my* first NHL trade—my dad, Tie Domi, was traded from the Winnipeg Jets to the Toronto Maple Leafs. When one of your parents is an NHL player, it feels normal for hockey to be a big part of your everyday life. Before I could even walk, I was soaking in the life of a professional hockey player.

My time in Winnipeg was brief, and the few childhood memories I have of the city are taken mostly from photos, like the one of Hall of Famer Teemu Selanne holding me right after I came home from the hospital. Today, on the NHL website, my hometown is listed as Winnipeg. That might technically be true, but after my dad's trade, I spent most of my childhood growing up in Toronto and Mississauga.

It was almost like I was made for the rink. When I was just two years old, my mom brought me along to my older sister Carlin's skating lessons. Carlin and I were fourteen months apart, so even at that young age, I wanted to do everything that she did, including learning to skate. During her lesson, I would stand at the boards with my face pressed up to the glass, occasionally waving or banging on the boards to get Carlin's attention.

The teacher noticed my excitement, and eventually she suggested to my mom that I join the class.

"Mrs. Domi" the instructor said, "it looks like Max can't wait to learn how to skate. We have room in the class if you'd like to bring him next week."

"Thanks for the offer," my mom said. "But Max is only two and a half. I thought kids had to be three to sign up."

The instructor looked carefully at my mom. "Sorry," she said. "How old did you say Max is?"

My mom wasn't usually one to break the rules, but lucky for me, she didn't have time to take back the words before they slipped out.

"Three," my mom said quickly. "Max is three."

The following week, I stepped onto the ice for my first lesson. There were groups of kids all across the rink, and each one had their own teacher and a small designated area of the ice. The instructor went from one kid to another, showing us how to stand up and balance on our skates. While I waited for my turn, I kept myself busy making snow angels on my back or wriggling on my belly, pretending to be a fish. I waved to my mom watching from the stands, a giant smile plastered on my face.

It didn't take very long before I was up and moving. Once I was, the poor teacher couldn't keep me still. I wasn't satisfied with staying in my little area. I wanted to skate all the way around the entire rink, just like I'd seen my dad do. To say I was happy is an understatement. I had found the place I was meant to be, and I loved it.

Learning to skate was the first step, but it didn't take long until I was begging to play hockey. I wanted to wear equipment like my dad did and be a real hockey player. There weren't any hockey leagues for three-year-olds, though, so my parents put me in a program called Hockey 101. It was really just a skating lesson, but we all wore equipment and there were nets on the ice. That was good enough for me.

Just before the end of each lesson, the instructors would set up a game. Or, at least, what three- and four-year-olds thought was a game. One of the kids in my class that year was Scott Laughton, who went on to play for the Philadelphia Flyers. Scott was a year older than me, and he'd figured out a few things that I was still working on. Like which net to score on. I must have only understood the part about putting the puck into the net, because after shooting on one net, I'd grab the puck and skate back to the other end to try and score on that goal, too. It was a bit of a learning curve, to say the least.

While I loved playing hockey when I was a kid, I didn't have the patience to actually watch the game. Whenever I arrived at Maple Leaf Gardens with my mom and sisters, I couldn't care less about the game on the ice—I'd run to the back of the room where I could play mini-sticks with the other kids. My dad would come out of the dressing room after the game all cleaned up and showered, while I would be covered in sweat from running around for three hours.

I still remember details about the hallways and equipment rooms in Maple Leaf Gardens. While I waited for my dad on practice days, I would spend most of my time hanging out with the equipment staff. I often hopped in the laundry cart sitting in the hallway, and the Leafs' equipment manager, Scotty McKay—who was like an uncle to me—would give me a push down the sloping, ramped hallway.

"Faster!" I'd yell as the cart picked up speed. I would be laughing like crazy as I went buzzing down the ramp. It was better than going to an amusement park!

Sometimes, I even got to go on the ice. I was still really young, so I spent most of the time lying in a snowsuit in the crease, throwing pucks into the empty net.

3

A few years later, the Leafs started playing at the Air Canada Centre. The family room at the ACC basically became our second living room. I preferred to watch from the rink, rather than at home, for one reason: they had the best cookies ever. Every game, there was a tray of sugar cookies, each in the shape of a maple leaf with a player's name written on it in this wicked chocolate icing: Sundin, Domi, Tucker, the whole team. The cookies were soft but not squishy, and the icing was lightly covered with this powdered icing sugar. I am deadly serious: they were the perfect cookies. I would literally race to the room to grab my favorite "Sundin" ones—I thought they tasted better, and I would take as many as I could hold. The other one I liked was the "Alex Ponikarovsky." He had one of the longest names on the team, and I knew that the more chocolate they put on the cookie, the more icing sugar would go with it. Plus, I liked Ponikarovsky as a player and he was a great guy, so it made the cookies taste better.

I was disappointed when my dad's hockey season ended each year. Not because we had to stop going to the rink, but because it also meant the end of my hockey season. But I would quickly be distracted by everything else happening during the summer. My second-favorite game was lacrosse. I loved the intensity and speed. I would have played only lacrosse all summer, but my dad was big on soccer. He thought it was a great way to stay in shape, so I also played on a team in Woodbridge.

Growing up the son of an NHL player was a little different. Most places I went, I was called by my last name. I absolutely hated it. My dad was an icon in Toronto, and I admired him. I wanted to be a pro hockey player, but I didn't necessarily want to be a player just like him. Even as a young boy, I didn't want to be just a Domi or "Tie's son"—I wanted to be Max. I wanted people to know me as my own person.

Don't get me wrong—I loved spending time with my family. And most of my day-to-day was the same as anyone else's. My parents would drive me and my sisters to school, take us to our after-school activities, and hang out with us on the weekends. Because my dad traveled so much during the season, though, it was often my mom I spent the most time with.

At my hockey games, most of the other kids had their dad in the dressing room helping them to tie their skates, while my mom helped me with mine.

Having my mom with me at the games was a big help. With my dad, it was hockey, hockey, and more hockey, before, during, and after every game. My mom was a completely different story. She always had a peaceful attitude, and she knew how to keep me relaxed if I got too worked up. "Have fun out there," she said to me before each game. Afterward, if I had a bad game, she'd just smile at me and say, "Don't worry about it, Max. You made some great passes today." She could always find a silver lining.

My mom was always there for me and my sisters. Every day she was the perfect example for us, showing us how to appreciate everything we had, and how to treat others with respect and compassion. These were important lessons for me, because the hockey world wasn't always the kindest.

When I was eight years old, I started playing AAA hockey with the Toronto Jr. Canadiens in the Greater Toronto Hockey League (GTHL). I was so proud to be on that team. We got jackets with our team logo on the arm, and I wore that thing to school every single day. It was easy to tell which cubby was mine outside the classroom—it was the one holding a Canadiens jacket with the right arm turned inside out.

The Canadiens were a minor atom team, and I was a year

younger than everyone else on the team. At first I was a little afraid about having to play against the older, bigger kids. But I wanted to prove to them that I could earn my spot on the team, and it felt even cooler that I was playing against kids who were older than me. I still felt I had something to prove. People were constantly telling me that I was getting special treatment because of my father. Everywhere my sisters and I went, we had to deal with that.

It followed me on and off the ice. The next season, when I was nine, I stayed at my own age group and switched organizations to play with the Toronto Marlboros. I specifically remember one game when the score was lopsided. The game got out of hand, and a bunch of us were sent to the penalty box. As I was sitting in the crowded box with my teammates, a dad of a kid on the other team approached the outside of the box. He started yelling at me and banging on the glass to get my attention. I tried to block out the things he was saying and focus on the game, but he wouldn't stop. Finally, the game ended and I was able to skate away to the far side of the rink with my teammates' stares following me the whole way. My teammates were shocked at the way the man had singled me out. I just wanted to pretend it didn't happen, but one of my teammates, Jordan Subban, decided to tell my mom what had happened.

"Mrs. Domi," Jordan said after the game, "that man made Max cry. He was swearing at us in the penalty box. He said the only reason that Max was on the team was because of who his dad was."

When I reached my mom, she could tell I was upset. I tried to act as though I was fine, but my mom could see the confusion on my face. The truth was that I didn't understand why that man had been so angry at me. I was used to other kids saying things like that, but I had never heard a parent make comments like that.

My mom pulled me aside and crouched down in front of me.

"Max," she said, "there is no reason for an adult to ever act that way or say those things. What that man said is untrue and inappropriate. My only explanation is that sometimes, bad kids just grow up to be bad adults.

"Unfortunately, there will always be people like that. But you need to understand that you can't change what other people do or say. All you can do is control how you deal with it. You have to rise above it."

It always stung when people accused me of getting a free pass just because my dad was a hockey player. My whole life had revolved around making it to the NHL; to me, there was nothing else that mattered. I felt that if I made it to the NHL, I would have succeeded in life. But I wanted to get there my way, on my own merits.

I was still a long ways off from a hockey career, though. If I'd had my choice, I would have quit school right there and then and just played hockey all day, every day. But my parents constantly drilled into me that I had to train my brain the same way I trained my body. I was an okay student. I could pick up things quickly, which helped. But if I was disinterested in something, I had no motivation to learn it. My number one concern at that time was just playing hockey, so if there wasn't a puck, stick, or net involved, I probably wasn't interested.

From grade three to grade seven, I went to Upper Canada College. I loved the school, but I spent most of my classes wondering, *When's recess? When's lunch? And when I am getting out of here to go to practice?*

I never had to wait long for my next round on the rink. Most weeks, I would have a two-hour practice on Monday. On Thursday, the team would have a one-hour practice, and then we would typically play games on Fridays and Sundays.

As a kid, then, Tuesday was the worst day of the week. Each Tuesday, all I could think about in school was that I had nothing to do that night or the next. At least on Wednesday I could tell myself that I had practice the next day. But Tuesdays were tedious.

To ease the boredom, I spent a lot of time in our garage on Tuesday nights. I would set up my net in front of the garage door, strap on my Rollerblades, and crank up the music. I'd spend hours in there, visualizing the game-winning goals I would score, and working on my stickhandling and shooting.

That time in the garage was great practice, and that was where I truly fell in love with working on my game. My mom didn't want me using a puck in case it ruined the walls, so I fired tennis ball after tennis ball at the net. The balls were light, and I would rip them as hard as I could to see how much power I could get. I sent balls all over the garage—they'd bounce off the net, off the back wall, off my parents' cars. I didn't give it any thought, until one day, when a friend came over to play some pickup. I took a shot, and the ball bounced off the post and onto the hood of my dad's car.

"Oh, my God!" my friend shouted. "Are we going to get in trouble?"

I gave him a look. "What do you mean?"

"You hit the car," he said. I could have sworn he was almost in tears.

"So what? That happens all the time. The ball doesn't leave a mark."

"So what?" My friend's jaw dropped open. "That's a Ferrari."

Turns out that all those years I'd been bouncing tennis balls off of the hood of a Ferrari Spider. Needless to say, I didn't tell my dad about hitting the car that day. Or the hundreds of other times it happened. To be honest, the car could have been a minivan, for all I knew; I was more concerned about perfecting my slap shot than protecting the car.

When you play AAA hockey, you need to practice. A lot. If I was going to take the next step in my quest to become a pro hockey player, I needed something more than scrimmages in the garage.

That was when I truly started to appreciate how lucky I was to have a dad who played in the NHL. My dad took me everywhere with him, from lunches with business partners to visits with the media to the rink. His philosophy was that the more I saw, the faster I'd learn.

"You can learn something from anyone in this world," he told me.

He was right, and just getting to be around some of his team-mates helped me think about things differently—not only hockey, but even just how to act around other people.

I knew I was lucky to have the opportunities that I did, but I was a shy kid, so most of the time when I went into the dressing room I would sit quietly and just listen. Most of my dad's teammates—Alex Mogilny, Gary Roberts, Joe Nieuwendyk—were famous in my friend groups, so I didn't want to seem too childish or overeager around them.

I didn't have anything to worry about. In fact, I thought all of my dad's teammates were genuinely big fans of my team the same way I was of theirs. Every time they saw me, they'd ask how my team was doing—I thought it was totally normal for a guy like Darcy Tucker to care about the standings in my Peewee League.

All of the guys were so generous with their time. Bryan McCabe would often come by where I was sitting and crack a joke to make me laugh. Tomas Kaberle always stopped to ask how I was doing.

Wade Belak was a gentle giant who was always asking about my family—he was a generous, kind person every time I saw him. And Matt Stajan was one of the younger guys on the team, so I related to him more and I admired his game.

One day, Curtis Joseph gave me an autographed picture, which I immediately hung on my bedroom wall. It was signed: "To Max, all the best. Curtis Joseph. PS, you still can't score on me! (Maybe one day)." So many nights, as I went to sleep, I would look at the photo and say, "One day, I'm going to score on CuJo."

As amazing as those guys were, though, there's no question that Mats Sundin had the biggest influence on me when I was young.

Mats would have a little smirk on his face whenever he saw me. "Hey, Maxie," he'd say, using his nickname for me. "How are you, buddy?"

Just hearing those words was enough to make my day. Mats was my favorite player—he was like a god to me.

"I'm good, thanks," I would say quietly.

"How's your season going?" he asked one day.

"We're doing all right."

"Scoring a lot of goals?"

"Kind of. I like passing more than shooting, though."

Mats smiled. "That's a good instinct to have. A great pass can feel as good as scoring a goal. Just remember that sometimes, though, the goalie is waiting for you to pass, so you might need to just shoot the puck."

That wasn't the only time a Hall of Famer told me that I needed to shoot more. A couple of years after Mats passed along that advice, Mario Lemieux said to me jokingly, "Max, in the NHL, they don't pay you for assists."

To be honest, I often heard the same sorts of messages from my dad. But he'd figured out that sometimes, he could get his message across better if it came from one of his Hall of Fame–bound friends than from his own mouth. Still, every single time I talked to one of the guys in the league like that, I would pick up a valuable lesson. Sometimes it was a hockey lesson, and other times it was a social one. I saw how the guys interacted with me and with each other in the room. I would blend into the background and pick up on the little cues, like how guys joked with each other versus how they acted when the coach came in.

One night, as I was leaving the ACC late with my dad after a game, I glanced down the hallway to the workout room. Almost everyone else had gone home, but Mats was in the gym alone, going full-blast on the stationary bike. He was so locked in that he didn't even see us go by. He was just giving it his all, sweating head to toe. I realized that if I was going to follow in the footsteps of a guy like Mats, I would have to work just as hard.

Every now and then, my dad would take me for a skate on the main ice, and if I was lucky, Mats would join us. On a few rare occasions, he would even come watch one of my games. Those were the coolest times for me. I could feel the pressure those nights, knowing that Mats was watching me play—I didn't want to let him down.

I loved it when the stakes were high during a game. When I was ten years old, I traveled out to Edmonton to take part in the Brick Tournament as part of an all-star team of kids from Ontario. This was a huge minor hockey tournament—for a ten-year-old kid, it felt like I was playing in the big leagues.

Each game, we would skate onto the ice like it was an NHL warm-up—there would be music blaring and the crowd would be cheering. Everything felt more intense: the crowds, the pressure, and the plays. There were mascots on each bench, and the games were broadcast by a local TV station. It was the first taste I had of how emotional hockey could get, and I wanted more.

I only scored one goal in all the games we played, but I ended up leading the tournament in scoring; all my other points came from assists. I was always a pass-first kind of player; I still over-pass to this day.

Of course, my dad noticed how I played. After our first game at the tournament, he took me aside.

"You can see the ice and pass better than anyone, Max," my dad told me. "That's a gift. Make sure you use it."

On a two-on-one in the NHL, most times you shouldn't be looking to pass—it's a shoot-first kind of league. But as a kid, my brain was hardwired to get more satisfaction from setting up one of my teammates than by scoring. I could see how happy each of my teammates was when they scored, so I kept setting them up for goals. Giving a guy a tap-in goal on a two-on-one always made me happier than scoring the goal myself.

On the flight back home, I thought back to that glimpse of Mats on the stationary bike. Even though we had made it so close to winning the tournament, we had fallen short. As a team, we felt we could be stronger. As an individual, I knew I had to be. *I want to be better,* I thought. *No, I want to be the best.*

If hockey hadn't already taken over my life before that point, it did then. By grade eight, any preoccupation I might have still had for school was completely replaced by hockey. The only courses I really enjoyed were the arts, especially drama. Acting in front of a group during a skit never bothered me. But if I had to read in front of a group of people, the butterflies would start dancing in my stomach and I'd be sweating from nerves.

To make my projects easier, then, I always brought things back to hockey.

"Max, what are you working on?" my mom asked me one evening as I was doing my homework.

"An English essay," I said. "I have to give a speech tomorrow."

"What are you going to talk about?"

"Mario Lemieux." She could barely stop laughing.

I needed something that would make my life easier, because 2006 ended up being a tough year for me personally. In June 2006, my dad retired from the NHL. Then, in September, not long after I turned eleven, my parents split up.

I was in the back of my mom's car as we drove up to our cottage, when my mom got a call from a friend of hers. I was in the backseat, and my mom wasn't saying much, but I could hear her friend talking quietly. All of a sudden my mom started breathing heavily, and she pulled over for a few minutes to gather her thoughts. My sisters and I stayed quiet—we knew something serious was going on, but we weren't sure how to react. Eventually, my mom explained what was happening.

I didn't cry when she told me and my sisters the news. I didn't cry when, a few days later, we talked about having to move. I only cried when I saw my mom cry. That hit me hard. My mom is the bravest and toughest person I have ever met in my life, and it was hard to see her cry. And there was absolutely nothing I could do—I felt helpless.

For a year prior to my parents' divorce, I'd had a recurring nightmare. In it, my parents got divorced and my sisters and I had to split up to live with them. I'd wake up from those dreams terrified that it would become a reality. *It's just a dream*, I'd told myself. Now it was a reality.

For a while I wondered if there was anything I could have done to prevent their divorce. I think a lot of kids wonder about that. Both of my parents assured me and my sisters that it wasn't about us, but it was hard not to let my imagination wander.

It was hard for my family to manage during that time. It became even harder when the newspapers and other media started to cover the divorce. Every detail became public. We felt like we had no privacy.

To help me get over my parents' divorce I did what I always do in tough times; I played hockey. Whenever I was stressed out, I would go down to the basement and start to stickhandle a puck or a ball. I began to look forward to practices and games not just as a fun time with friends, but as a necessary escape. As soon as I had a stick in my hand and was skating around, it seemed like there was nothing in the world that could faze me. I wasn't a kid who was bored at school or whose parents were getting divorced—once again I was just that happy two-and-a-half-year-old skating laps around the rink.

While my parents' divorce sucked, we all adapted. It was the little things that I found the hardest. I was used to coming out of the dressing room and finding both of my parents waiting for me. We'd talk about the game and I'd relive every moment, listening to my dad's advice and my mom's encouragement mix together. Now, as part of my postgame routine, I would go over and talk to my mom on one side of the rink, and then go over to talk with my dad on the other. It felt like I was walking from one world to another.

There were some rough patches, to be sure, but my parents were both dedicated to making sure my sisters and I had everything we needed. After a while it almost seemed like my parents were jointly raising Carlin, Avery, and me; they were just living in different houses. When it came down to it, my family was healthy and we were all a part of each other's lives—we had all of the important things in life. We settled into our new normal, and I went back to worrying about not much beyond playing hockey and having fun. Outside the change in our family, I was lucky in that I didn't really have a care in the world.

But all of that was about to change not long after my twelfth birthday.

2

NEVER PANIC

In November 2006, I got sick with a fever. I remember vividly just how terrible I felt, because I didn't usually get sick, and when I did, I could kick it pretty quickly. But this felt different. My parents had split a few months earlier, and although I'd kept my emotions in check, I felt worn down.

My mom was concerned, so she took me to our family doctor. Dr. Strachan had been my doctor for years, and he was also a long-time minor hockey coach in Mississauga—he had photos all over his wall of kids he'd coached. Dr. Strachan gave me a full checkup, and he even had some blood work done to be extra safe. When my blood tests came back, they hadn't detected anything serious, so we figured I had a nasty virus of some sort. I needed to rest and take care of myself. So my usual life of school and hockey continued, although I still definitely wasn't myself.

Of course, none of that stopped me from playing hockey. No matter how crappy I felt, I refused to miss my activities, which probably didn't make for a speedy recovery. I didn't care how bad I felt, though—I told myself I had to fight through it. I was playing for the AAA Toronto Marlboros, and I didn't want to fall behind.

"Max, are you sure you want to go to practice tonight?" my mom would ask.

"Of course! I'm totally fine," I would reply, even though I felt like garbage.

By the following spring, though, I had lost some weight, and my mom noticed I was a little paler than normal. My parents worried I might be wearing myself out, but I was so active that neither issue seemed alarming. And it wasn't impacting my play—I was having a great season.

At the end of the season, I was invited to take part in a hockey camp hosted by the HoneyBaked Hockey Club, an AAA hockey team in the Detroit area. The coach's name was Mike Hamilton, and he ran an incredibly competitive program. Each year, Mike organized an amazing three-day training camp, and he invited top players from across Canada and the United States to Detroit—some guys even flew in from California and Dallas. I got an invite, and so did Darnell Nurse and a few other guys I played with and against in the Toronto area at the time. The whole idea was that we would learn more about the game, push each other hard, and have some fun doing it. So, needless to say, there was no way I was missing that camp.

Mike brought in specialized coaches to do training and drills, and they even brought an expert to talk to us about mental toughness. It was a big-time experience for a bunch of twelve-year-old kids. I loved it, and it felt first class, with the quality of talent on the ice and the quality of the coaching we were receiving.

Mike and the coaches pushed us hard for three straight days. Each evening, as I piled my bag into the back of my mom's car and headed back to our hotel, the only thing I had the energy to say as I slumped into the front seat was, "I'm so tired." Neither my mom nor I thought too much about how tired I was—the coaches had us players going full-tilt the entire time we were there, so it was understandable that I'd be tired.

When camp ended on the third day, my mom and I jumped into the car. We hit play on one of her favorite CDs—Shania Twain—and hit the road back to Toronto. As we drove down the highway, I felt my mouth getting drier and drier.

"Mom, I'm so thirsty," I said. "Can we stop?"

My mom pulled over at a gas station and bought me a sports drink, and as soon as I cracked it open, I guzzled the whole thing down.

We took off again, but as soon as we hit the highway, I had to pee so badly that I felt I was about to burst. I tried to hold it in, thinking it would pass, but it got worse and worse—every bump in the road was painful.

"Mom, I need to pee."

"Max, we just got on the road. Can't you wait a bit?"

"No, Mom."

We got off at the next exit, and I rushed to the closest bathroom. As I walked back to the car, I started to feel my mouth go dry again. My tongue was like a piece of wood in my mouth.

"Mom, I'm thirsty again. Can I get another drink?"

I drained my drink again the moment I opened it and hopped back in the car. *That's better*, I thought, figuring I could catch a bit of sleep on the way back. But a few minutes later I was hit with the need to pee again.

This went on the whole drive back to Toronto. One minute I felt as though I'd swallowed a desert, and the next I felt like I'd been holding my pee for hours. I felt guilty every time I asked my mom to pull over, but every time it felt like I was going to explode.

It took us forever to get home, and by the time we got there, my mom figured something was up. She called my aunt Trish and told her all about what had happened. The first words out of Trish's mouth were, "Oh, my God."

"What's wrong?" my mom asked.

"It could be nothing. But everything you're saying are symptoms of type 1 diabetes. Max needs to see the doctor first thing tomorrow."

My mom didn't want to alarm me, so after she spoke with Trish she sat me down and calmly explained that the next day we were going back to see Dr. Strachan.

In Dr. Strachan's office, we explained what had happened on the trip back from Detroit. Dr. Strachan listened patiently, then excused himself and came back with a testing kit.

"Max, I'm just going to take a drop of your blood for a quick test, okay? Can I see your finger, please?" he said, holding up a small, rectangular tool with a screen on it.

He made a small prick to the end of my finger, and I watched a drop of blood appear. There was a white strip inserted into the top of the device, and I watched as Dr. Strachan held it up to my finger and the strip sucked up the tiny droplet of blood. Dr. Strachan gave me some gauze to hold against my finger, and then he studied the device for a moment. It let out a beep, and then Dr. Strachan turned to me and my mom with a serious look on his face.

"Your blood sugar is very high, Max," he said. "It looks like you might have type 1 diabetes."

My mom and I looked at each other. For her, time stood still for a second as our entire future as a family shifted. But I had no clue what the diagnosis meant. So I said the first thing that came to mind.

"Can I still play hockey?"

Dr. Strachan's face broke into a wide smile.

"Of course you can! Do you know who Bobby Clarke is?" he asked. I gave him a blank look. "He was one of the hardest-nosed players to ever play the game. And he has diabetes. If he could play in the NHL with type 1 diabetes back in those days, you can do it now."

I was relieved—my dream of playing in the NHL was still alive. *Good*, I thought. *That's the end of it.* Little did I know, there was a long road ahead.

"Right now, though, you need to head over to SickKids Hospital," Dr. Strachan said. "I've called them and set up everything for you. You need to head there now."

"Why do we have to go now? Can't we wait a little bit?" I asked. Up to that point, visits to the doctor had been straightforward—they found out what you were sick with, gave you some meds, you went home, and you got better. Going to the hospital made this diabetes thing sound more serious than I wanted it to be.

"I'm afraid not," he said gently. "You and your family need to talk with the doctors there as soon as possible."

"I know it's scary, Max, but everything's going to be all right," my mom said.

I was scared, but it wasn't because of the diabetes. Going to the hospital meant getting tests, and getting tests meant needles. And I hated needles. They were my biggest phobia—a fear I shared with my dad. I once tried to skip school just so I could avoid having a flu shot.

I knew I didn't have a choice, so we left Dr. Strachan's office and drove immediately to SickKids. On the way over, my mom called my dad and told him about the diagnosis. After a couple of minutes she handed the phone to me.

21

"Your dad wants to talk to you," she said.

"Dad, who's Bobby Clarke?" I asked.

My dad started laughing. "Bobby Clarke was one of my favorite players growing up. He was the captain of the Philadelphia Flyers. He has diabetes, but he's tough, he could score—he did everything."

"Dr. Strachan says I can still play hockey."

"Of course you can."

I passed the phone back to my mom and looked out the window. As we pulled into the hospital parking lot, I told myself that my parents were right—nothing would stop me. I would get through this.

The second we arrived at SickKids, my life as a person with type 1 diabetes officially began. For the next week or so, I was at the hospital every single day. We arrived at seven a.m. each day, bracing ourselves for the long, grueling series of tests and meetings that would follow—not an easy introduction to living life as a person with type 1 diabetes.

I started by seeing a specialist named Dr. Pearlman. He was a short, older guy with gray hair, and he was the head of a team of doctors, nurses, and dieticians who would be with me each day for the endless laundry list of tests, needles, and classroom training sessions. Every day in the hospital was like an extreme hockey practice—drill after drill, each one focusing on a different skill with a different expert.

Dr. Pearlman and his team started right from the beginning and explained what exactly the disease was. The amount of information we were trying to take in was overwhelming. I'd learn about one thing, like how to use a glucose meter—the device that tests my blood sugar level—but before the lesson had sunk in, I'd be off to the next meeting, where we'd cover something entirely different, like how insulin injections worked.

The specialists' main goal was to teach me how insulin worked in my body. I had never even heard of insulin before I was diagnosed, so I didn't have a clue what it was supposed to do. I could barely make sense of the medical talk going on around me, but the specialists broke it down for me.

"In simple terms," Dr. Pearlman told me, "insulin is a hormone that your pancreas produces." He gestured to the top of his abdomen to show me roughly where the pancreas was. "Insulin helps your body use sugar from the food that you eat. It helps your body absorb or use glucose for energy. But in type 1 diabetes, the body can't produce enough of its own insulin, so your body cannot use the glucose in the food you eat. Without insulin, your sugar levels could build up in your blood, which could be very dangerous. So you have to give yourself insulin every day—including every time you eat and before you go to bed—to keep yourself safe."

My point person at SickKids in those early days was a nurse named Ana. She ran the ship, and she gave me a handbook full of exercises that would help my parents and me manage everything that I ate. Ana also worked closely with my dietician, Anita, who made sure that I understood just how crucial it was to eat the right food and be aware of what I was putting into my body and what it might do.

"It will be important to learn Max's insulin-to-carbohydrate ratio. And you'll have to count his carbs carefully," Anita told my parents. "Max should eat a healthy diet just like everyone else. The difference is that he needs to make sure he calculates what he is eating and then gives himself the appropriate amount of insulin that he requires."

"Mom, what's a carbohydrate?" I asked. I knew that foods like bread and pasta had something mysterious called "carbs" in them, but I didn't know what they were exactly, and I had no clue you could count them.

After reading the handbook, I had to pass a number of tests. For the first one, I was given a plate full of fake food—a banana, some bread, and mashed potatoes. I had to count the carbs on the plate, and then figure out the right amount of insulin I would need to give myself with that food.

"What if I'm at a birthday party? Can I have cake?" I asked.

"Of course," Ana told me. "You're like everyone else."

"There's nothing that you can't eat," Anita added. "You just have to do everything in moderation."

Ana and Anita, along with the rest of the team at SickKids, emphasized that message a lot—they made it clear that it was important that I continue my life as normally as possible. Although my life was now different, I was still allowed to be a kid and eat cake and other good things. The dietician put it simply for my parents: "You wouldn't let your other children eat candy or cake constantly, so neither should Max."

Learning about carb-counting was one thing, but even with the most careful counting, there was always the chance that something could go wrong. The next step, then, was for me to learn about the danger signs and what to look for if, as the doctors called it, I "went low."

"You might feel shaky, weak, or sweaty," the doctor said. "If it gets worse, you could find your speech slurring or your vision blurring."

That doesn't sound so bad, I thought.

"It's important you pay attention to those warning signs, Max," the doctor continued. "If you don't and your blood sugar keeps dropping, you could pass out and potentially even have a seizure. Worst case scenario, you could go into a diabetic coma and die. I don't want to scare you, but you have to know the risks. It also means you should have simple sugar—like juice—with you so that you can treat your lows before they get serious."

That news hit me hard. A week before, all I'd worried about was whether we'd win our next game. Now the doctors were telling me I was living with a potentially deadly disease. As the seriousness of my type 1 diabetes sank in, all I could wonder was, *Why me?*

In between all of these educational sessions, the doctors were constantly doing blood work to monitor my blood sugar. Short term, I had to pay attention to the risks of high and low blood sugar levels. If I didn't, there were potential long-term dangers, like eye, kidney, and nerve damage. All of those were preventable if I maintained normal blood sugar levels, though, so the doctors reinforced how important it was that I monitor my blood sugar levels regularly. For a little while it just seemed like an interruption, as though this were a onetime sickness that would pass. But after a few days, the reality sank in— I would be testing my blood and giving myself insulin every day for the rest of my life. This wasn't an interruption, this was my new normal.

We spent our downtime between meetings in a tiny waiting room near the doctors' offices. One day we were hanging out waiting for some test results to come back. We had TSN on the TV in the background, and a feature story came on. I wasn't paying much attention, but suddenly my dad said, "Check it out—it's Bobby Clarke!"

I knew from what my parents and Dr. Strachan had said that Bobby Clarke was a big deal, but I didn't realize until that moment that he was a legend in the NHL. The opening montage included a clip of Clarke raising the Stanley Cup, smiling with no front teeth and long hair. They showed a montage of his best goals and hits. *He's tough as nails*, I thought. It reminded me that, although things weren't easy, I could get through it.

After several days of intense training and studying with the team at SickKids, my family and I were sent on our way. I was completely drained, physically and emotionally. The doctors and specialists at SickKids had taught us so much about the disease. But everyone reacts differently to type 1 diabetes, so it's like anything in life—you can only really learn by experiencing it.

We came home with our arms full of charts, including carb-counting posters and warning charts that displayed the crucial symptoms of low and high blood sugar levels. During those first few days when we came back home, everyone was in a bit of a fog as we tried to figure out how I would live life as a person with diabetes outside the hospital.

My sisters, mom, and I had moved to a new house not long before I was diagnosed. The week before I had gone to the camp in Michigan, a woman had come to our door with her two young kids. Mrs. Suzanne Ross introduced herself as our neighbor across the street. She said they were collecting donations for the Juvenile Diabetes Research Foundation (JDRF), and she introduced her two boys, Noah and Jamie, who both had type 1 diabetes. My mom donated some money to the foundation, and she paused, as the idea of how difficult it must be having kids with diabetes registered with her.

A week later, on one of the mornings when we were about to head to SickKids, my mom ran into Mrs. Ross's husband.

"Sorry, we've only met briefly," my mom said. "But you're Noah and Jamie's dad, right?"

"Yes. I'm Larry," he said.

"I met your wife recently while she was collecting sponsorships for the upcoming JDRF walk," my mom said. "You aren't going to believe this, but Max was just diagnosed with type 1 diabetes."

For a moment there was silence, and then Mr. Ross gave my

mom a hug. They may have been newly acquainted, but suddenly they shared an undeniable bond as parents of a child living with type 1 diabetes.

"It's hard to describe what you're in for," he said quietly, "but we are here to help you."

Mr. and Mrs. Ross promised to share whatever information they had about living with the disease. It meant the world to my family to know that we had friends like that we could rely on.

While the team at SickKids had been so helpful and given us the essential information about living with type 1 diabetes, there was still so much to learn that was individual to my body alone. By talking with people like our neighbors and experimenting day by day, my family and I were able to slowly learn how my body worked and what "my" diabetes looked like. There are many aspects of living with diabetes that doctors can't prepare you for—you just have to experience them. Every person's body is different and so is every person's lifestyle, so there's no exact "how to guide" in managing the disease.

My body changed quickly in the weeks following my diagnosis. Now that my family knew what was wrong with me and how to deal with it, I started to gain back my weight. Every time I tested my blood, I appeared to be fairly stable. More than once we said to each other, "We've finally got the hang of this." It seemed that things wouldn't be so bad after all.

The team of specialists at SickKids had warned us this might happen. After a diabetes diagnosis, most people go through what's called a "Honeymoon Phase." In simple terms, it's the period after a diagnosis when your body is still producing a small amount of insulin and you need to take fewer insulin shots. Unfortunately, it doesn't last forever. We'd been warned that we would all know when

I was coming out of that phase. And when that happened, things sure changed.

Once you experience what it is like for your blood sugar to go low, you realize just how dangerous it is. When I go low, it brings out the worst in me. I get very cutthroat and mean. It can get so bad that I don't want to talk to or see anyone. I also get incredibly hungry when I'm low. In a lot of ways, going low is the same sensation as if you're really drunk. You wobble around like you don't really know where you are, and you have fuzzy vision. Your anxiety can go through the roof, too. Sometimes I'll be in such a haze that I'll catch myself staring at an object for ten minutes straight.

Going high wasn't any better. When my blood sugar levels spike, my palms and feet immediately get sweaty. My head starts pounding, and I'm constantly thirsty, even though, at the same time, I also constantly have to pee. I don't feel loopy like I do when I go low, but I still get irritable and snap at anyone around me.

When I was first learning how to recognize all these symptoms, I was afraid of going high or low—it all seemed so far out of my control. But it was so much worse for my family, who had to deal with my nasty moods. The problem with diabetes is that there is no tried-and-true mathematical formula for telling you the exact right thing to do in every situation. For example, if I was low one day and had a juice box with 15g of carbs, fifteen minutes later, I would be fine. But the next day, if I was low again, that same juice box might not be enough. Lucky for me and my family, I could usually tell when something wasn't right. But my mom wasn't taking any chances.

Each night, my mom would set her alarm for three a.m. so that she could test my blood. It didn't matter how tired she was or how much else she might have done for me and my sisters that day—she was always there, looking out for me and making sure my blood sugar hadn't dropped in the middle of the night. I was just entering my teens, so most times, when my mom woke me up, I'd grumble, "Mom, leave me alone. I just want to sleep!" But it never stopped her from making sure I was safe. My mom is a special person.

Toward the end of the school year in 2007, my class was scheduled to go on a big field trip north of the city. It was going to involve a long bike ride and a short flight in a small plane—we were going to study mapping as part of our geography class. It seemed like a cool way to learn to me, and I was excited for the unique experience. But my dad really didn't want me going on the field trip. He was worried it was too soon after my diagnosis for me to be going away like that.

My mom worked at convincing my dad.

"He has to be able to do the same things as other kids," she said. "We can't smother him in bubble wrap or have him feel afraid."

My dad eventually agreed. But there was a catch—my mom insisted that she come along to make sure nothing went wrong.

The school drove us all in a bus to Norval, where we rode our bicycles along country roads for what seemed like forever. When we finally got to our destination, we would board a small Cessna plane that would fly over the countryside so we could study the lakes and forests.

As we biked, I felt myself getting more and more tired. It wasn't a difficult ride, so I knew it wasn't a question of fitness—it was my diabetes. I refused to stop, though. I didn't want to make a scene or be the reason everyone had to pull over. So I cracked open one of the many juice boxes I had with me and kept pedaling. The farther we went, the harder it became to keep my focus. I was getting antsy and was just about to snap when finally our destination came into sight.

As I put my bike away, I felt a glimmer of hope through my sour mood. It was the first time I'd gone low while exercising, and I'd made it through.

My mom was the only parent on the trip, but she did a great job of hanging in the background. She waited at all the check-in stops along the bike ride, just in case I needed anything. She was like a ninja—nobody even knew she was there.

I was still a typical kid, trying to pretend that I didn't need my parents for everything, but the truth was that I was so relieved to know that my mom and dad were there for me like that. And it wasn't just my parents who helped me—my sisters were also a huge help. Looking back, I'm so thankful for everything my sisters Carlin and Avery did for me over the years. Both of them were living their lives and trying to reach their own goals. But even while they were doing their own thing, they were patient and compassionate as we figured out how to manage everything. I don't know where I would be without my sisters.

That whole summer of 2007, I was under a microscope. Somebody was always watching over me. But I was still playing soccer and hockey, and as a family we did all of the things we would normally do—day trips in the city, barbecues, visits with friends. I never wanted to miss any sports, and to their credit, my parents never told me that I couldn't play or that I had to stay back from anything. I knew my parents were stressed, but we sat down one day and had a serious conversation about what they needed from me.

"Max, we want you to be able to do all the things that your friends and any other twelve-year-old would do," my dad said.

"But if you're going to do that," my mom said, "you have to be smart and always be prepared. You need to always have your glucose meter with you, as well as juice and snacks in case you need to treat low blood sugar."

"You have to be disciplined about checking your blood and taking your insulin. Don't take any chances," said my dad.

"You know how important this is and what the consequences are," my mom warned. "As long as you follow all the steps for managing your blood sugar, there's nothing you can't do."

What I wanted to do more than anything else was play hockey. My parents were constantly thinking about my health and how to help me be a normal kid. But most of the time I was thinking, *Having to poke myself with all these needles sucks, but at least I get to play hockey.*

There were lots of kids my age who were diagnosed with diabetes and still played sports. But competing in AAA hockey was sort of pushing the boundaries. I had gained back most of the weight I'd lost when I was sick, but now I had to get back in my routine.

At first I forgot things all the time. I had a big backpack full of everything I might need throughout the day—insulin, snacks, juice, my glucose meter—but I hated carrying it. I didn't want to stand out or look different from any of my classmates. I'd try to forget that I had diabetes and act the same as any other kid. But, like it or not, I wasn't the same.

My diabetes was constantly reminding me of that. I would be walking from one class to another and then realize I hadn't tested my blood for a few hours. That meant I would panic, not knowing what my blood sugar was, which only made things worse.

To help protect me, my parents sat down with my teachers and the administrators at my school to explain my situation. My mom went out and bought a ton of juice boxes, which she gave to the school. After the meeting with my parents, every teacher kept a little row of juice boxes right behind their desk. It gave me—and the teachers—a lot more peace of mind knowing we had that safety net there in case of emergencies. A few of the teachers in particular—Max Perron, David Bacon, and Richard Vien—went above and beyond to make sure that I felt like I never had to ask for help.

My mom was always the most on top of everything. She taught herself more about the disease than anyone else in my family, and she made sure I was prepared for everything.

That was so important in the early days of my disease. Early on, after I was diagnosed, I could never tell what my blood sugar level was. It took time to learn how to listen to my body. Some people can learn a new thing right away. That was never me. It took me a few months at least before I got a handle on how many blood tests I needed throughout the day.

My friends were really curious about my new routines. One day, at recess, my friends Rob Adamo and his brother, Victor, came up to me while I was testing my blood.

"What's a good number?" Rob asked.

"It depends on what I've eaten, how I'm feeling, that kind of thing," I said.

Rob looked at the glucose meter. "Can I try?" he asked.

I showed Rob how to prick the tip of his finger and deposit a bit of blood onto a fresh test strip. A few seconds later, the screen on the glucose meter lit up.

"4.4," I said, using the Canadian measurement system for blood sugar levels of millimoles per liter (mmol/L), the equivalent of 80 milligrams per deciliter (mg/dL) in the U.S. system.

"Is that good?" Rob asked.

I laughed. "It's good. It means you don't have diabetes."

Years later, Rob told me that, in that moment, he realized how much more I had to think through and consider my every choice on an everyday basis. At the time, though, I was just at the start of my learning curve. The more I learned about how my body responded to things, the easier my day-to-day became. I needed that, because hockey was starting to really pick up. Right after I was diagnosed in the spring of 2007, I attended tryouts for the AAA Don Mills Flyers. I made the team, which meant I would be leaving the Toronto Marlboros and starting the next season with the Flyers in the fall.

I had worn the number 13 my whole life because of Mats Sundin. I patterned my whole game after Mats, so I wore 13 in honor of him.

But when I went to Don Mills, it hit me that I was playing for the Flyers—Bobby Clarke's team. Bobby Clarke wore number 16, and the number was available when I started with the team. The more I thought about it, the more I wanted to switch my number so that I could honor Bobby Clarke. But I was worried that I would upset Mats if I changed numbers, so I decided to run it by my dad.

"Dad, do you think Mats would be upset if I switched numbers?" I asked.

My dad laughed. "I don't think he would mind at all."

"Are you sure? Can you ask him?"

Of course, Mats was fine with it. As soon as I heard that, I decided that I would wear number 16 from then on.

Early into my first season with the Don Mills Flyers, I was in Whitby, Ontario, for the annual Silver Stick Tournament. The tournament is a big deal for youth—it brings out teams from across Canada and the U.S.—and the crowds are usually packed.

Between a couple of my games, my mom was sitting in the stands when she noticed some people approaching a man for autographs. When the crowd parted, my mom saw who it was: Bobby Clarke. She waited for a break in the crowd, and then she went up to him.

"I don't usually do this, Mr. Clarke," she said. "In fact, I have never done this. But is there any way you could come and meet my son?

He has type 1 diabetes and he plays for the Flyers—he even changed his jersey number recently to honor you. He wants to play in the NHL someday, and I know he would love to meet you. Is there any way you could come talk to him?"

I was in the dressing room when one of my coaches came over.

"Max," he said. "There's someone here to see you."

Then Bobby Clarke walked through the door. I was in awe. Neither of us said a whole lot—I didn't know what to say. But we had our picture taken and he wished me luck in the tournament. A minute later, he was gone.

It was a blur, but in my mind it was the coolest thing that had ever happened to me. I was so fired up, as though nothing could stop me. Knowing that Bobby Clarke had done it—he'd not only made it to the NHL but been one of the best who played the game— gave me confidence that I could do the same.

Even now, there isn't a day that goes by when I don't think of Bobby Clarke; I wouldn't be where I am today without his inspiration. At the time, between my diagnosis and hockey getting more serious, my days of living a stress-free life were over. I knew that the responsibility of taking care of my diabetes was now with me 24/7. I was going to have to think carefully about every single thing I did, not just to make it to the NHL, but just to survive. But with Bobby Clarke's number on my back, I was ready for whatever came next.

3

ALWAYS HAVE A PLAN

Once I got over the shock of being diagnosed with type 1 diabetes, I didn't have any doubts at all that I wanted to keep playing hockey—it was what I wanted to do more than anything. The rink was my escape. As soon as I stepped on the ice, all I had to focus on was hockey; everything else just melted away.

Still, I was worried about how far I could push my body. I was scared of what would happen if I went low. I didn't want to miss a shift during a game. Anytime my blood sugar started to go low, it affected my play—when I started missing passes that I usually didn't miss or screwing up simple drills, I'd know it was coming. Soon after, I would feel my skating slow down, and my stickhandling would become sluggish. It would make me frustrated, which would only make things worse.

As a person with diabetes, everything you do has to have a plan. When you wake up, you go through your checklist—your mental one, and, for me personally, a physical one—as you work your way through what will be going on that particular day. You visualize what you need to get through it, where you're going to be, and what to bring with you. Preparation is the key.

Of course, I didn't have that level of planning when I was thirteen years old. When I was off the ice, I'd often go to my buddies' houses, where all my friends would be playing street hockey or basketball. I'd get there, and it would hit me that I didn't have my test kit with me, so I couldn't monitor my blood sugar.

Forgetting your test kit is a crucial mistake for a person with diabetes, so you'd think it would be the one thing I would never do. If you're at the movies and you go high, or you're playing basketball in someone's driveway and you go low, you need to know right away so that you can solve the problem.

But there are days when you wake up and you're not thinking clearly, and training your brain to remember all of the little things takes a lot of practice. Every time I forgot my kit, I'd tell myself that I had to take my condition more seriously and be better about remembering the one thing I was supposed to do every day. Gradually I got better, but not without making a lot of mistakes.

Whenever I left the house, my dad was all over me, checking to make sure I had everything I needed.

"Max, take another juice box with you."

"Dad, leave me alone—I feel fine."

"You might need it later."

"I'll be fine."

Sure enough, I would pay the price for my stubbornness later in the day. I would be in the middle of class or in the car, and my blood sugar would go low. *This is not good*, I'd think as I got the sweats and started to feel light-headed. *I wish there was some juice around here.*

In those first few months after my diagnosis, I was so shy that I didn't even feel comfortable testing my blood in the hockey dressing room or in class at school, because I didn't want to draw attention to myself. Whenever I absolutely had to, I tried to hide it.

The only person I wouldn't mind testing myself in front of was Darnell Nurse. He was one of my closest buddies and I knew I could trust him. The first time Darnell saw me testing my blood in the dressing room, he asked what I was doing.

"It's no big deal," I said, trying to play it cool. "I just have to do a quick test."

"Do you have diabetes?" Darnell asked.

I looked up in surprise. "You know about diabetes?"

"Yeah, man. My grandparents both had it. But I didn't think anyone our age could have it."

I was relieved to find someone who knew what diabetes could look like. But I was still self-conscious about it around people. A few months later, I was at the movies with my friends Robert and Charlie. During the movie, I had to test my blood. That alone was quite the process in the dark—the pop of the test kit container sounded deafening in the quiet theater, and it took me longer than usual as I fumbled around with the lancet, trying to fit the tip of my finger to the test strip. When I finally finished, my glucose meter showed I was a 2.7mmol/L (roughly 47mg/dL), which was too low. I stood up and was about to go to the snack stand to get a drink, when Robert stood up instead.

"I saw you're low—I'll get you a juice," he whispered. I sat back down, grateful for having such good friends.

After the movie, I thanked Robert again for stepping out in the middle of the movie.

"No worries, man," he said. "I knew you were excited for that movie."

"I know, but I didn't want anyone else to miss it," I said.

"You don't have to hide your testing from us," Robert said. "It's kind of cool."

"What are you talking about?" I said. "It's embarrassing. Can you imagine if I had to pull out my glucose meter in front of a girl?"

Robert and Charlie looked at each other. "Actually, that'd be great," Robert said.

"I can't think of a better icebreaker than that," Charlie said with a grin.

I should have been comfortable testing myself in front of anyone and everyone—I know now that there is nothing to be ashamed of when it comes to our health, physical or mental. But I wasn't comfortable, and that was a problem. The number one rule when you have diabetes at a young age is to communicate—you have to let everyone know what is going on.

My parents knew that none of that would stop me from playing hockey. But they also knew the kind of person I was and that I had a habit of forgetting things. So my mom made sure to tell the coaches of the Don Mills Flyers about my diabetes and what to look out for.

My coaches worked hard to educate themselves about my diabetes, and they were always dialed in. But knowing the warning signs didn't mean much if I didn't speak up. If I didn't tell the coaches I was feeling unwell, they wouldn't know there was a problem. And I never spoke up. I never wanted to be seen as different than anyone else or draw attention to myself. I wanted to fly under the radar and do my thing. I already had enough attention because of my dad; I didn't need any more. Extra attention just made me uncomfortable.

In my first few practices with the Flyers, I tried not to say anything. I didn't want anyone to think I was looking for special treatment. But that approach didn't last long.

My coaches quickly learned that if I started to gaze into space, or if I wasn't making sense with my words, or if I was easily turning pucks over in practice, something was wrong. They'd quietly come over and suggest that I test my blood sugar levels, and sure enough, I was usually low.

I didn't realize how much easier it became once I made sure everyone around me was kept in the loop. When I finally started letting my coaches know what was going on, they were completely understanding. They would tell me, "Your health is number one. If you don't feel right, don't ever feel bad about just going to the bench until you're good to go."

Sometimes, though, it was just a matter of grinding through whatever I was facing. When I was fourteen, I played on a summer hockey team called the Regional Express Gold. Coach Dalt ran the team, and his practices were insane—some of the hardest I've ever had. He was strict, to say the least—Coach Dalt was also a corrections officer.

I knew some of the guys on the summer team, but most of them played in a different league than me in the fall, so I'd never seen them before. Because I didn't know anyone that well, I wasn't comfortable telling them about my diabetes. I didn't want them wondering why I was the one guy who stopped partway through drills to go to the bench and drink Gatorade. The way I saw it, if someone ever bailed on a drill in practice, it was a sign they couldn't take it. Needless to say, I didn't want to be that guy.

Sure enough, we were in the middle of a brutal practice, and my blood sugar started to go low. As I waited in line for one drill, I could feel my energy lagging. *I don't want to be here anymore*, I thought. It wasn't a thought that would ever cross my mind when my levels were normal.

I had already finished the one Gatorade that I had brought, and I didn't have anything else with me. The combination of the active insulin and the intense practice had caused my blood sugar level to plummet, and the Gatorade wasn't enough. For the first time ever, I started looking at the clock, hoping the practice would end.

Coach Dalt screamed at us, "Go hard!" He used to call me "Boomer." I have no idea why. As I struggled down the ice, he kept yelling, "Let's go, Boomer! Move it!" I was in so much pain that I could barely think straight—I had to will myself to the end.

Somehow I made it through the rest of the practice. Afterward, I sat in the dressing room silently, feeling as though I was going to faint. It had been tough physically, but more than that, mentally I was completely shot. No doctor or nurse, no parent, no coach would ever have condoned what I did, but in that moment, I was trying to find my way and see how far I could go.

Moments like that showed me how much easier it would be to compete when I was fully prepared. At first it seemed overwhelming—I'd have to do this forever, after all. But the more I thought about it, the more I realized that if I just added a few more things to my checklist when I was getting ready, I could avoid all sorts of pain later on.

Treating my diabetes became part of my daily routine, like getting my sticks ready on a game day. The same way that I would never go on the ice if my sticks weren't taped properly, I needed to take the extra time to make sure my body was ready. And the same way that I would never pack my hockey bag without my skates, I made sure to never go to the rink without my test kit, insulin, and something to treat my lows. What had seemed like such an insurmountable challenge before suddenly became much more manageable. I just had to stay disciplined.

My parents had the same line of thinking. They were great about making sure that my diabetes never held me back from doing the same things as other kids. But they both drew the line when it came to parties. Their attitude was that, if I wanted to be a hockey player, they were going to invest a lot of time and money in me, and I had better take it seriously. My mom was a little looser about it. But my dad was incredibly strict.

When I was eight years old, my dad told me, "I am going to treat you like an NHL player. I will help you in every way I can. But you have to take this seriously."

That meant not just playing hockey, but training like an NHL player in the off-season. Luckily, I really liked running. It started when I was kid. One of my first trainers was Charlie Francis. Charlie was one of the best track-and-field coaches of all time. At times, though, it seemed as though Charlie was less coach, more wizard. If I wasn't running well, he would walk to me, pinch the skin on the side of my arm, and, if he didn't like the feel, he'd look at me and say, "You didn't drink enough water today." He was always right.

I loved working with Charlie, so I didn't see our training sessions as work. Still, I had to approach the sessions with the same level of discipline I brought to any game or practice. Training in general was a challenge. Different types of workouts—weight training versus cardio—taxed my system in different ways. And as a person with diabetes, changes in each energy system would affect my blood glucose in different ways.

On the days when I hit a wall on the track or didn't have a great day on the ice, I took my dad's words to heart and tried my best. There were ups and downs—a few times, I said, "Screw this, I want to go to a movie with my buddies. I don't care if I have a game tomorrow." My dad wasn't pleased when I pushed back like that, but I knew that he wanted the best for me.

About a year after I was diagnosed, my dad's habit of constantly checking up on me paid off in a big way.

I was home with my sisters one night, and my mom was out. My older sister, Carlin, was fourteen years old at the time, but Mom still had our babysitter Stacey come over just for some peace of mind.

I had been training at a park all day with a close friend of mine, John Doyle, and just after I came home, my mom gave me a big plate of pasta and a glass of chocolate milk. Before I ate anything, we counted the carbs to make sure we had it right.

Knowing I had all the food I needed and that I was all set up, my mom headed out. But after she left, I decided I wasn't hungry, so I only ate half the food she'd put out for me. The problem was that I still gave myself the same amount of insulin as if I had eaten all of it. I didn't realize it, but I'd just given myself way too much insulin, which would cause my blood sugar levels to go low.

After dinner, I went to go lie on the couch. Carlin, Avery, and Stacey assumed I was resting because I had been training all day.

Not long afterward, my dad called to talk to me. Stacey told him that I was sleeping.

My dad got nervous and told Stacey and my sisters to check on me right away.

They didn't know what the big deal was, but when Carlin tried to shake me awake, I didn't budge. They tried calling my name, clapping, and tugging my shoulders, but nothing worked—I just lay there semi-conscious.

My younger sister, Avery, started crying and Stacey, realizing that something was very wrong, called 911 and asked for an ambulance to come over immediately.

Meanwhile, Carlin understood that I was low and that I needed something to get my blood sugar up, so she ran to the fridge and got some juice, which she tried to get me to sip.

My dad was on the phone the whole time, asking what was happening. I slowly started to come to, and when I did, the first thing I saw was Carlin trying to give me a juice box. I was still kind of out of it, so I grabbed the juice box and whipped it across the room.

Carlin didn't give up, though. She tried to make me test my blood. I could barely hear anything—my brain was fuzzy and everything sounded like I was underwater—but I saw my test kit was on the table next to me. I grabbed it and threw it across the room, too, where it broke into pieces.

At that point, Carlin went to our neighbors across the street, Larry and Suzanne Ross, the couple with the two young boys who had diabetes. They ran across and took over the situation.

By the time the ambulance arrived, I was a little more with it and was feeling more like myself. I had been so low that I didn't remember anything that had happened. When Carlin told me about how I had thrown the juice and the glucose meter across the room, I was shocked.

The paramedics checked me out to make sure I was okay. Luckily, my blood sugar levels were stable and it was safe for me to stay at home. But if my dad hadn't called to see how I was feeling, my blood sugar would have kept dropping. It was a really scary incident, but we were grateful, because it could have been worse. My sister Carlin was a real hero to me that day.

That was the first time it hit home to everyone in our family that my diabetes was a potentially life-threatening disease. We had heard about scenarios exactly like this in our training at SickKids.

But, as with everything else about this disease, we were learning that until you experience what it is really like, you don't understand how bad it can be.

After my diagnosis, I had to return to the diabetes clinic at the hospital every three months for blood tests and talks with my doctor and nurses. It was routine procedure. They just wanted to see how things were going and make sure I was staying healthy. They would do blood work and review my blood sugar readings to evaluate a number of things, one of which was my A1C, or a three-month average of my glucose levels. The finger-stick tests I did multiple times each day let me know how my blood sugar levels are in real time, but the A1C gave the doctors an overall picture of my diabetes management.

The first few times, the appointments were nerve-racking. I would walk in hoping that nothing else would be wrong. After the first few meetings went by without a problem, the check-ins started to feel like a formality. Normally, I was in and out of them pretty quickly.

"Your blood sugar levels are a bit all over the place, Max," the doctor said.

"I know."

"Have you been testing your blood and counting carbs, like we talked about?'

"I have," I said. "It's just hard to manage it with all of the hockey I'm playing."

"I know it's hard. But it's also important."

Everyone at SickKids was great, but I was still young, and there were days when I wished that my appointments felt like less of a lecture. The meetings were starting to look as though they'd just be another one of those things I had to get used to, like testing my blood or counting the carbohydrates in my meals. Of course, it was then, just as I was starting to relax, that I was hit with another bombshell.

It was two years after I was initially diagnosed, and I was having trouble stabilizing my blood sugar. That wasn't always my fault, but it seemed to be an ongoing problem, even when I was doing everything right. My mom had read that it can be common for people with type 1 diabetes to also have celiac disease, another autoimmune condition. When we were at the clinic for one of my regular checkups, she discussed that possibility with the doctor, and he agreed that it could be the issue causing my unstable blood sugar levels. He ordered some special blood work to determine if there might be evidence of celiac. *Great,* I thought, when I heard the news, *more blood work.*

That was just the first step, though. When the initial blood work came back, it showed that there was a likelihood of celiac disease. When he saw that, the doctor ordered a scope test to confirm the diagnosis.

I didn't like the sound of that. The doctor assured me that it was a short procedure—called an endoscopy—that would allow him to see what was going on inside my gastrointestinal tract. He'd remove a small piece of tissue from the tract, which they would test to confirm whether or not I had celiac disease.

When I arrived in the examination room on the day of the procedure, the first thing I saw was a thin tube attached to what looked like a trigger.

"Don't worry, Max," the doctor told me. "This tube has a camera at the end of it. I'm going to use it to take a look down your throat, all the way to your stomach and intestines. It won't hurt. I will be putting you to sleep for a short time, and you won't feel a thing."

After the procedure, the doctor shared the results with us.

"Mrs. Domi, Max's esophagus is covered in ulcers. Has Max ever complained about his throat being sore?"

"No, never!" my mom said. "Max, you would have said something if you were in pain, right?"

"Of course," I lied. I had sometimes had trouble eating certain foods—stomach cramps and that sort of thing—but I'd figured it was just from the insulin or my blood sugar levels being all over the map, so I'd kept quiet.

"That's surprising, because this might be the worst case I've ever seen. It's clear—Max has celiac disease. His body cannot tolerate gluten, and it's causing damage to his intestines, which is why he can't digest his food properly. That's what would have made it so difficult to control your blood sugar levels, Max."

"What does that mean?" I asked.

The doctor smiled. "We will have to go through the foods you usually have—I'm afraid you won't be able to eat some of them anymore."

I started listing some of my favorite foods—pasta, bread, cookies—and my heart sank as the doctor said no to almost all of them. I was crushed.

"There is good news, though, Max," the doctor said.

"What's that?" I asked. I found it hard to believe.

"There are many gluten-free versions of the foods you like. So you'll still be able to eat a lot of your favorites."

The news helped a bit, but I was still bummed. After home and the rink, the hospital was becoming the place where I spent most of my time. It had been exhausting learning how to live with diabetes, and now that I had celiac disease to figure out, it felt like I was right back to square one. I didn't want to be a sick kid; I just wanted to be a kid.

Before we left the hospital, I asked my mom if I could go get a snack while she talked more with the doctors. I went over to the Tim Hortons nearby, and I bought a ten-pack of chocolate Timbits—my favorites. I could eat an entire pack and still want more. I figured they would cheer me up.

I ate the pack of Timbits, met up with my mom, and headed home. An hour later, I felt horrible.

"Max, what's wrong? What did you eat earlier?"

"I got a pack of Timbits," I admitted quietly.

That was the wrong answer. My mom dropped the hammer.

"Max, what were you thinking? You heard what the doctor said. I know it's hard, but you can't do things like that. Your health is too important."

From that day forward, I was on a full-blown gluten-free diet. The first few months were tough. Back then, not many food items were listed as gluten-free, and there were fewer options in general. In a lot of ways, learning how to deal with my celiac disease was harder for me and my family to figure out than diabetes.

Everything my parents knew about shopping for food and cooking had to completely change. After my diagnosis, my mom would spend more than three hours shopping for food. She would read the info on the back of every package, and if the ingredients weren't clear, she would call the 1-800 company phone number that was listed and ask them about the gluten content. Once we figured out what packaged food I could have, we were fine—we just bought the same ketchup or barbecue sauce over and over. But there was a huge learning curve at the beginning.

My mom even took lessons that my dad organized with a chef so that she could learn how to cook gluten-free foods. Some lunch meat from the grocery store contained gluten in its seasonings. To avoid that, she would cook a roast beef or a turkey and then slice it up into lunch meat with one of those machines you see at the deli.

I could control what I ate at home, but going out to restaurants was harder. I could no longer eat anything from Tim Horton's the way Rory and I used to devour donuts and butter-covered bagels. I'd learned my lesson from the Timbits, so from that point on it was just hot chocolate for me.

During hockey tournaments, the team would usually go out together for a big meal before the first game. The guys around me would be ordering pasta and garlic bread. Their food would arrive on the table, and my mouth would water at the smell. Then a chicken Caesar salad (no croutons) would appear in front of me, and I'd come crashing back to earth. A hungry fourteen-year-old feels like he can eat anything, so it took a while for me to get past jealously looking at everyone's meals.

Although I missed Tim Hortons and McDonald's and all that other food that kids love, the good news was that my overall health improved and my blood sugar numbers stabilized. Before my celiac disease diagnosis, my carb-counting had been all off. My parents or I would look at my plate and check the carbs on it, and then I'd give myself an insulin dosage based on that. But because of the celiac disease, my body hadn't been absorbing the nutrients properly, so no matter how carefully we counted my carbs, it was always slightly off. Now that I was all-in on the gluten-free diet, my diabetes became more manageable.

The spring after I was diagnosed with celiac disease, I went on a school camping trip. We were sleeping in big tents on platforms out in the woods—there were at least ten of us inside each one. Once we were all packed in with our sleeping bags and backpacks, there wasn't a lot of room to move around. I was having trouble finding a place for my bag—it had all of my diabetes supplies, so it was way bigger than everyone else's. But I'd learned that was no excuse not to have those supplies with me.

I woke up in the middle of the night. My blood sugar felt off, and I had to go pee. It was pitch-black, but I desperately had to get outside. I tiptoed over my sleeping classmates, trying not to step on anyone, which was hard, given how uncoordinated I could be when I was low. Luckily, I managed to make it outside and back without any problem. When I got back in my sleeping bag, I knew I had to test my blood.

I remembered that I only had one strip left in my test kit. I had more in my bag on the other side of the tent, but I had figured I would just refill my test kit in the morning. I tried to quietly test my blood in the dark, but I couldn't manage to squeeze out enough blood from my fingertip for the test strip to register it. When that happens, the glucose meter cancels the test. I quietly kicked myself for not having replaced my test strips earlier. I crept over to my bag and tried to find my replacements, but I was having no luck, and every rustle of the zipper sounded as though it would wake up the entire tent. Eventually, I gave up and went back to my sleeping bag, crushed a juice box just to be safe, and lay awake the rest of the night, waiting for the sun to come up.

A younger me might have just shrugged the whole thing off and moved on, hoping for the best. But I knew better. The next day, I vowed to make sure that I would stay on top of everything and ensure I had the supplies I needed. I would make sure to test my blood when it was light out, and before I went to bed I put my entire diabetes bag full of supplies beside me. Taken on their own, each of those little details didn't seem like much, but paying attention to them meant the second, third, and fourth nights in the tent were a walk in the park for me.

On the bus ride home, I felt grown up. I had encountered a problem caused by my diabetes, but instead of ignoring it, I'd figured out a way to take care of myself. I felt proud. *Maybe I'm finally learning how to live with this disease*, I thought.

There's no doubt I put my parents through a lot of stress when I was younger—it took me a long time to learn that it was okay to ask for help. I wanted to be a normal student and teammate. I learned the hard way that there's nothing wrong with testing my blood in front of the guys in the dressing room, or telling a coach that I might need a break during practice, or packing extra apple juice if I was staying over at a friend's house.

I just wanted to play road hockey, go camping, and hang out with my friends. But, unlike all my buddies, unless I was prepared for whatever life threw at me, there would be consequences. I wasn't like everyone else—and I was finally coming to accept that.

4

KEEP THINGS IN PERSPECTIVE

September 2010 brought with it most of the usual signs that fall had arrived—school started up again, the days were getting shorter, and my hockey season with the Don Mills Flyers began. But there was something different this year. Because this was my Ontario Hockey League (OHL) draft year.

It was the same concept as going into the NHL draft. It was the last year of minor hockey, and every game had scouts in attendance who were watching your every move. Everyone on my team wanted to play at the next level, so, knowing that every showcase tournament we were in was filled with scouts, the pressure was on to perform at every game.

That pressure just added to the demands I was already juggling from my diabetes. By this point I was well used to the day-to-day life of a person with type 1 diabetes. I had my routine, and every day I was learning to read my body's signs about how it was feeling. But there were still daily frustrations.

In one class early that year, a student brought in cupcakes for his birthday. Treats were being passed around the room, and I really wanted to have one, but they weren't gluten-free.

"Max," the teacher said quietly, trying and failing not to draw attention to me. "I'm sorry there's sugar in these cupcakes."

"I'm not going to have one," I said. "But it's not the sugar that's the problem, it's the gluten."

The teacher smiled knowingly, seemingly missing the point. "I understand what you're going through—my uncle has diabetes. He hated having to give up birthday cake."

I shifted my weight, trying to avoid the looks of my classmates. "Actually, I have type 1 diabetes, so I can still have sugar."

The teacher looked confused. "I see. Well, if you need anything, let me know."

People seemed to think that type 1 diabetes was like a peanut allergy, and that you had to avoid sugar entirely. More and more, I was realizing that most people didn't understand the difference between type 1 and type 2 diabetes. Type 1—what I have—is an autoimmune disease that's often inherited, and there is no cure for it. The cells in my pancreas that are supposed to make insulin—called beta cells—can't do their job because my body's immune system destroyed them. Because of that, my body creates zero insulin on its own. So I have to provide insulin from the outside, instead of my body releasing it internally. For people who don't have diabetes, their normal beta cells are sensing their sugar levels every minute. In my case, I have to poke my finger for a drop of blood to measure what my sugar levels are and where they are going.

These days, people with diabetes can wear a continuous glucose monitor that makes it easier to know where their blood sugar level is at all times. But giving insulin still needs to be done by the person, either with injections or through an insulin pump. As a person with type 1 diabetes, I can still have sugar. But if I don't eat the right foods or stay on top of my insulin, my life could be in jeopardy.

I have to constantly balance my blood sugar so that it doesn't get too high or too low.

Type 2 diabetes is a very different disease. With type 2 diabetes, a person's body makes some insulin, but it's not enough or their body doesn't respond to it properly, so the insulin that their body makes isn't as effective as it should be. Type 2 diabetes is not an autoimmune disease like type 1. Type 2 diabetes is more common in people who are inactive, overweight, and older, or who come from certain high-risk groups. However, it can also happen in children. People with type 2 diabetes also have to monitor their blood sugar levels and make sure they don't get too high. Some people with type 2 diabetes can regulate their disease through exercise and a healthy diet, but people with advanced type 2 diabetes usually have to take oral or injectable medications, including insulin in some cases. And no matter what type of diabetes a person has, controlling the blood glucose levels and having a healthy lifestyle are incredibly important.

I knew the difference between the two because I was living with the disease. But I wasn't the most patient with others who weren't as familiar with it. I was a typical teenager—I hated having to explain myself. *Why can't people understand the difference?* I wondered.

Because of that, I often had "Why me?" moments. The constant blood testing, the explanations, the carb-counting—most of the time it was just par for the course, but there were times when I felt sorry for myself and complained silently about how unfair it was that I had this disease.

But no matter how badly I felt for myself, things were put in perspective every time I walked through the doors at SickKids. Every three months, as I walked through the hospital to the diabetes clinic at the back, I would pass by kids who were hooked up to IVs or oxygen tanks that were keeping them alive. And yet, when I saw those same kids shopping for a teddy bear or coloring with their family, they had smiles on their faces. In those moments, I was reminded of how truly lucky I was and how, in the grand scheme of things, I didn't have much to complain about. I realized that life was precious, and I had to enjoy every moment with the people around me.

Everyone talked about my diabetes like it was a struggle or a challenge, something that I suffered from. But I wasn't suffering. And the more I thought about it, the more I saw my diabetes as a positive. I told myself that I had my diabetes to thank for my preparation and discipline; it was helping me to mature quicker than many of my friends. I realized those kinds of things would make me a better athlete. Having diabetes was a part of who I was, but I would not let the disease define me. I would define the disease.

That improvement in my mind-set was crucial, because every variable in my life could play a factor in affecting my blood sugar. Even today, stress can make my blood sugar go high and then crash. Nerves or anxiety, whether on a game day or an off day, can have the same effect. Too much activity one day can throw off my blood sugar as much as if I am not active the next. Most of the time I was thinking about those diabetes challenges in the context of hockey—I always wanted to be able and ready to play. But that year, I discovered that there were other sports that had an effect on my blood sugar. Among people with type 1 diabetes, certain sports or activities can have an outsized impact on their blood sugar levels, causing them to go really low or really high. For some, it's golf. For me, it's basketball. I could guarantee that whenever I played some pickup basketball with my neighbors, my blood sugar would go low. Sometimes I'd use this to my advantage—exercise typically lowers a person's blood sugar level, because the body burns sugar for energy. So, if my blood sugar was high, I'd go run around outside and shoot some hoops, and my blood sugar levels would drop right down. The same went for swimming—anytime I was in the water, the exertion of swimming and my body keeping itself warm would make my blood sugar go low.

I would often play basketball with friends, and they started to learn than, even when I was locked into a game, I would notice when my blood sugar levels were going low, so we'd stop to take a juice break and allow my blood sugar to climb back up. Today, continuous glucose monitors make it a lot easier to measure where blood sugar levels are and where they're heading, but they weren't an option for me at the time.

Another curveball came from being sick, or even just dehydrated. I had to keep myself constantly under the microscope. When I was sick, insulin interacted differently with my system. I typically found my blood sugar levels going very high, and it was a struggle to get them back down again. If my blood sugar levels went off—if I made even the slightest mistake—it could affect me for the next twenty-four hours. Sometimes if I had a severe low, it would take so much out of me that I would still feel drained two days later.

With all the games we were playing and all the intense practices we were having, I couldn't afford those kinds of mistakes. There had been times in the past when I'd just tell myself I needed a day off from being a person with type 1 diabetes. But that year, with the OHL draft coming up, there was too much on the line. I was willing to do anything to make sure I played.

At times I might have taken that too far. When I was younger, my dad wouldn't let me play if my blood sugar wasn't in a certain range. A person without diabetes typically has a fasting blood sugar level anywhere between 3.9 and 5.5mmol/L (70–100mg/dL). After a meal, that number can spike up to around 7.8mmol/L (140mg/dL), but people without diabetes have a balance between their insulin (which lowers blood sugars) and glucagon (which raises blood sugars), so they keep themselves in balance. Almost everyone has felt edgy and hungry if their blood sugar is dropping. Usually that's not because the person's blood sugar level itself is low. Rather, their body feels the falling sugar and tells the person that food is needed. But in those cases, even if the person doesn't eat for hours, nothing bad happens because the body's natural systems kick in, quickly regulates their blood sugar levels, and maintains the balance.

For people with diabetes, though, the highs and lows are much more dramatic. Their insulin isn't balanced, and any dose can be too much, causing their blood sugar to fall way too fast. Sometimes, that fall in blood sugar can be so fast that the person doesn't even know what's happening and they can lose consciousness. No doctor is holding your hand, telling you what dose of insulin to take. It's always a calculation based on what you ate, how much you're going to exercise, and what your blood sugar level is.

My optimal blood sugar level on a normal day off was anywhere between 5mmol/L and 8.5mmol/L (roughly 90mg/L and 154mg/L on the American measurement system). If I was in that range, everything was great. But on game days, there was a much wider range to my numbers, partially because my entire mind-set was focused on the game ahead. Sometimes, my blood sugar level on a game day could jump up as high as eighteen. In those periods of intense or prolonged exercise, I had to be careful to interpret my blood glucose readings really carefully. The high number on my glucose meter reading could be partly caused by the effects of adrenaline and other hormones, not just high glucose, an effect called a "false high." When that happened, I still often had to give myself insulin to bring my blood sugar level down, but I had to use some guesswork to make a smaller correction than usual.

When the game was about to start and I tested my blood, if I was around a 7 or 8, I could almost guarantee that I would have a good game that night. But if I was a 3 before the game, no matter what I told myself, I knew that if I was going to play to the best of my abilities that night, it was going to demand a lot more mentally and physically. Every game, I learned a bit better where my limits lay and how far I could push them in a healthy, safe way. I'm still learning that to this day.

Even when I was that low, though, I didn't want others to know it. I wanted to be on the ice, no matter what. If my dad or one of the assistant coaches caught my blood sugar at anything under 4.5, they would force me to sit for ten minutes until my level came back up. It was the right call for a parent and coach to make. But ten minutes is an eternity during a hockey game to sit there and not play.

I didn't want those sorts of things holding me back. I wanted to stand out that year and catch the OHL scouts' attention. How else was I going to stay on track for the NHL?

"How's your blood sugar, Max?" an assistant coach would ask me right before a game.

"It's a six, I'm good to go," I'd say. In reality, I could have been as high as 20 and I would have foolishly said the same thing, because I wanted to play.

My parents had my best interests at heart, and after a few games where I went low, they caught on that I wasn't being honest about my blood sugar levels. They said to everyone on my team, "Whoever is with Max, don't just ask his level—make sure you look at his glucose meter yourself."

I tried to work around the system. I'd reassure my coaches that I had just tested by blood and that I was fine, or I'd try to avoid their check-ins.

Looking back, I can't believe that I thought that was a good idea—it was so dangerous, and I wouldn't recommend that anyone ever try it. But when I was in my mid-teens, playing hockey and getting to the next level meant more to me than always being on top of my diabetes.

That mentality is crazy, and scary for a parent. And I can only imagine how much it screwed up my performance on the ice—I have to admit that, if I'd had perfect blood sugar when I was a minor midget, I would have been a lot better and a lot more consistent. But at the time, I was putting hockey ahead of my health.

Thankfully, that was about to change. That year, my parents and I were connected with a doctor named Bruce Perkins. Bruce was special. For one, he had type 1 diabetes himself. He understood what it felt like to go low. He also understood wanting to push boundaries. Bruce had always done things that were challenging for people with type 1 diabetes—hiking, scuba diving, cycling. He was a well-respected physician, too, so my parents and I sat down with him and asked him for some advice.

"Max, I expect your blood sugar levels are all over the map," he said when we met.

I was shocked. Because of the competitive level of the hockey I was playing, it was hard to keep my blood sugar levels dialed into an even level. I dreaded the days where I had to go into SickKids and look at the unimpressed expressions on the faces of the doctors and nurses as they reviewed my data.

"Yeah, it can be hard sometimes," I said.

"I get that," Bruce said. "Actually, I think I'm a little high right now."

"Really?" I asked. I couldn't believe that even a successful doctor who specialized in diabetes wasn't always perfect when it came to his blood sugar levels.

"It happens to all of us," Bruce said. "I have so much respect for what you're doing. I can't even skate backwards."

"I want to keep playing hockey," I said.

"And you will. We will figure this out," he said. "It will take some time, but we'll get there. One thing I will say, though, is that no matter how much you want to play hockey, you're only going to be able to do that if you put your health first."

I appreciated Bruce's approach—I got the sense that he wasn't there to lecture his patients, but to help them find a new way forward.

I listened to Bruce's advice, and I ended up having a good year with the Flyers. Our team made it all the way to the OHL Cup final, a showcase tournament for the top minor hockey teams across the region.

Leading up to the OHL draft, I had all sorts of different voices— my parents, teammates, classmates, scouts—telling me what I should do next. I changed my mind every day. Monday I was going to the OHL. Tuesday I was convinced I was going to play in the NCAA. Wednesday I was looking at the USHL. I was getting different advice from my mom, from my dad, from my teammates, from my friends at school, everyone. I knew I was going somewhere, I just didn't know where!

More important, though, I was learning how to get my on-ice temper under control.

During a hockey game, guys will chirp, or insult, you to make you mad and get you off your game. When I was a young kid, that kind of stuff would frustrate me way more than it should have. A guy would slash me in the corner or shadow me wherever I went on the rink, and I'd quickly get upset. I would never complain to a ref or a coach about what the other guy said. I would take care of it myself. Often, though, that meant I'd take a dumb retaliatory penalty by slashing the guy back or pushing him as we went to the bench.

I saved all of my complaints for my parents after those difficult games. They would listen patiently, letting me get it out of my system, before answering. My dad always gave me the same response.

"All those people are just trying to get under your skin," he said. "If they didn't say anything to you, then you'd have a problem, because it would mean you're not good enough to get that kind of attention. If they're chirping you, that means you're doing what you need to do to be successful. All they're doing is trying to get you off of your game."

My dad told me to watch Sidney Crosby. He would make me watch what Sid went through every game and how he fought through the chirps or the hacking against his wrists, all in the name of being the best player in the league. Everyone was trying to get Sid off of his game, but Sid just did his thing. He took a lot of abuse, and I admired him for that.

Bit by bit, my skin started to thicken. I learned that that kind of talk meant nothing. I knew that, whatever happened on the ice, I had to maintain my focus on what I needed to do that game. As soon as I reacted and took a retaliatory penalty, I lost, and the other guy won. And I always wanted to win.

Of course, that was easier said than done, because my temper could get the better of me. There was a player on the Mississauga

Senators named Matt Donnelly who drove me crazy. Driving to games against the Senators, I would get more and more worked up knowing that I was going to have to battle with him.

The most common chirps I heard from Matt and other guys like him who were trying to get under my skin were about my dad. Hearing a guy compare me to my dad, or tell me that I wasn't him— or even that my dad wasn't any good—could really throw me off.

Matt and I crossed paths years later, and he turned out to be a great guy—he even came to my defense a few times. Eventually I came to realize that even when someone was trying to get me going on the ice, he might not be a bad guy off of it; that was just the role that he played for his team. When you let those kinds of mind games get to you, it turns a team sport into an individual sport. And when it comes down to it, that's what matters—the team. You do whatever you need to for the guys on either side of you.

In February 2011, I had the chance to take part in the Canada Winter Games in Halifax. The tournament was kind of like a mini Olympics for youth—it featured competitions across several sports, and each province sent a team to the competition. I was playing for Team Ontario in the hockey portion. It was my first time representing something bigger than my local hockey team—now I was representing my province. The first time I pulled on my jersey, I was filled with awe and pride.

We had a fantastic team—Jordan Subban was on it, and so were Darnell Nurse and Bo Horvat. Every guy in the room was one of the best—if not *the* best—player on his minor team. I'd gone head-to-head with a lot of them before, and some of us had long-standing rivalries, but we put all of that aside to focus on winning together.

Our coaches were clear—each of us would have a role on the team, and we were expected to do our job. It was the first time I had ever been part of a team where everyone had been told so clearly to park their egos. Looking around, I could see that the other guys took the message as seriously as I did.

I also recognized that managing my blood sugar was going to be more important than ever during the tournament. Luckily, I had a familiar face to help me out. The trainer with Team Ontario was Dr. Johanna Carlo, or Dr. Jo, as I called her. She was also the trainer for the Don Mills Flyers, so she knew all about my diabetes and how I should be handling it.

Each night, Dr. Jo set an alarm so she could wake up and check my blood sugar levels. Like clockwork, Dr. Jo would come into the room at three a.m. and wake me. My roommate was Darnell Nurse, and he never complained once about the disruption. We never talked about it, but I was always so thankful that he never made a big deal out of this—it helped me stay calm and meant I never felt like I had to hide anything.

Dr. Jo was a great trainer, but she'd only ever seen me at the rink. Now she was with us twenty-four hours a day for the tournament, and some of my methods for staying balanced came as a bit of a shock to her.

One night, Dr. Jo checked my levels on the glucose meter and frowned.

"Max, you're really low," she said. "I'm a little concerned about this."

"It's all good, Dr. Jo," I said. I reached to my bedside table, grabbed a package of Swedish Berries, and started devouring the candy. Dr. Jo seemed surprised—it wasn't the most scientific solution, but when we checked my blood sugar a little while later, I was fine.

Candy couldn't solve the problem every time, though. A few

nights later, my blood sugar was low again, but this time it was stubborn. No matter what I tried, my blood sugar wasn't coming up. We had a game the next day, so I couldn't afford to stay low. After an extended period of time, Dr. Jo was starting to get worried.

"I'm sorry, Dr. Jo," I said. "I must have given myself too much insulin."

"It's all right, Max," she said. "But I think it's time we called your mom."

"No, please don't," I said. It wasn't anything against my mom—at that age, I just didn't want help from anyone. "I'll be fine. My levels will come up."

"You don't know that, Max. We have to be safe."

I kept trying to negotiate, but Dr. Jo wasn't having it. She texted my mom, and the next thing I knew, my mom was running over from her hotel in the middle of the night with toast and peanut butter for me. My mom had come prepared—her hotel room was stocked with snacks and foods just for me. There weren't as many gluten-free options readily available back then, so she'd even brought a pasta maker and griddle in case she needed to make gluten-free meals for me.

In the end, I was thankful that Dr. Jo contacted my mom. With her help, we managed to get my blood sugar levels back to normal, and I was able to play the next day.

While my mom was very involved, she was also good about staying out of my way—that's why she was staying in a different hotel than me. She didn't want me to feel that there was a parent always hovering over me wherever I went. She knew I was a normal teenager—I was stubborn, and I didn't want to listen to anyone. And I was extremely hotheaded when it came to people telling me what to do. I wanted to do whatever *I* wanted to.

As a person with diabetes, though, I didn't have the luxury of wallowing in those teenage feelings. I had to treat situations different than everyone else. Even if I wouldn't have admitted it at the time, deep down a part of me knew that by taking the extra measures my parents were constantly talking about, I could make my life so much easier.

The tournament was a learning experience for me on the ice, too. I was entirely average that tournament. It had nothing to do with my diabetes. It was more the case that I was out of my comfort zone and was playing at the highest level of hockey I'd ever competed at. We ended up losing in the semifinals to a British Columbia team that had future NHL players such as Nick Petan, Curtis Lazar, Sam Reinhart, and Shea Theodore. As I packed my bag after our final game, I thought about what the tournament meant for my dreams of making the NHL.

You have to pay your dues to make it to the big leagues. That means different things to different people. For me, that meant I was going to have to make more sacrifices.

That was a daunting thought. Luckily, I had my friends to help me escape. I had a group of hockey buddies I'd hang around with, and we had our own way of communicating. Telling our parents we were "going to a movie" actually meant spending three or four hours walking around the mall, hanging out with girls.

Sometimes, though, I couldn't escape, or things were too intense and I needed a break. In those situations, I couldn't always turn to my friends. I was the kind of kid who held a lot of stuff in, and I didn't easily share with a lot of people. When that happened, I would turn to the two people I trusted most: my sisters.

Avery was always a trooper. During the fall, Carlin took horseback riding lessons up in King City. My mom would drive Carlin up there after school, then take me to hockey practice in Toronto, and then do the whole round trip again to pick us both up. The whole time, Avery would be sitting in the back of my mom's car, doing her homework or catching up on sleep. She never complained, though—sometimes she was so quiet you almost forgot she was sitting back there. And her unselfishness never went unnoticed in my mind.

That was Avery, though. She was the biggest supporter of everyone in the family, always up for anything. She was really into fashion and had a creative mind. She was an unbelievable athlete in her own right, too, who played basketball and volleyball, and who ran track and field.

Carlin was a hard worker. She was the oldest of the three of us, and she was like an extra parent at times. Sometimes Avery and I pushed back against that, but we knew Carlin had a big heart, so we usually followed her lead.

All three of us had such different personalities, and we relied on each other growing up. Whenever I wanted to play hockey in the driveway, I'd try to get one of them to play goalie. When Carlin said no (as she often did), Avery would be the chump. She didn't have much of a choice, and more than once, I accidentally sent a ball flying toward her face.

Don't get me wrong—we fought a lot, too. But when push came to shove, we always had each other's back. That's how we were raised. If one of us was struggling, we knew we could go talk to either one of our siblings and they'd help us get through it. We trust each other in every aspect of everything, and we're always there for each other, no matter what.

I was thankful for that, because on top of the diabetes and the hockey there was something else that demanded sacrifices from me: my dad.

My dad was always hard-nosed. If he wanted something done his way, he was getting it done his way. If I went to a movie or hung out with friends and stayed up too late—even if it was a Saturday night and I didn't have a game for the next three days—he would be all over me.

"You can't do that!" he said one night after I got home an hour later than I said I would. "That's not how it works. That's not how you're going to get to the NHL, and that's not how you're going to behave here. These are the types of sacrifices you're going to have to make, Max."

As a kid, it could be hard to keep up with my dad. He was like the cartoon Tasmanian devil, always moving a mile a minute. Sometimes his energy came off like anger, and after more than one of his infamous postgame critiques, I would almost be in tears. I could score three goals in a game, the team could win, and he would still be more concerned that I had turned over the puck in the first period or that I'd extended my shift too long. He didn't want me to ever get complacent.

I understood he wanted the best for me, and as I got older and grew a thicker skin, I learned how to deal with the criticism. I'm convinced that every little thing my dad said helped me out in the long run. I always wanted to be by his side, whether it was in the car, on the ice, or even just going to lunch with him and seeing how he interacted with his business partners.

My dad was extremely intense even when he was eating lunch. As my dad talked, he'd scribble notes on a napkin for me to take home with me. I would just sit there quietly, too shy to make a fuss, trying to process what I was seeing and hearing. He never really coached me on the ice, so meals became one of his favorite coaching venues.

"See this ketchup bottle, Max?" he asked one meal. "That's you. The mustard is your winger. The salt and pepper are their D-men. Got it?"

I nodded shyly.

"When you see the mustard go to the net and pull the salt and pepper back, you've got a few options," he said, grabbing a knife and fork to show how I could either hit one of my trailing defensemen with a pass or take a shot on net.

"Dad, can you pass the defenseman, please?" Avery asked from across the table, pointing at the salt.

As much as my dad liked to give us his own advice, he was also the one who taught us that a truly smart person knows when to ask for help.

In the middle of my season with Don Mills, I was struggling. There was a guy on one of our rival teams named Dalton. No matter what, I could not beat Dalton on a face-off. One day, my dad took me to the Windsor Arms Hotel in Toronto.

"Why are we going to a hotel, Dad?" I had asked him earlier.

"I just got off the phone with Mark," he said. "He's in town, and he's going to help you with your face-offs."

"Mark who?" I asked.

"Mark Messier," he said. "Go get two sticks and a puck."

My dad took me into the hotel restaurant, and sure enough, Mark Messier was sitting there at a table by himself. I was intimidated, to say the least. I tried to get my brain to tell my legs to move closer, but my brain had shut down. Mark was a legend, and one of the most respected leaders in the history of the league. My dad had always told me, "You want to be like Mark Messier. He's a winner."

My dad and Messier had been teammates on the New York Rangers, and they'd been friends ever since. They caught up for a bit, and I just sat beside them, staring in disbelief at Messier. Finally, my dad got to the point.

"Mark, Max needs some help winning face-offs. Got any pointers?"

Messier turned toward me and broke it down simply. "You've got two options on a face-off: You can go with speed or power. You can't do both. You're a strong kid, right?"

"I think so," I said quietly.

"All right, then. Hold your bottom hand on the stick really tight. When the puck drops, don't try to beat the other guy to it. Instead, keep your hand low and come underneath the other guy's stick. If you can stay strong on your stick, you'll beat him clean every time."

The next time I faced Dalton was during a playoff series that year. We lined up across from each other for the opening draw, and as I approached the circle, I slid my bottom hand toward the blade of my stick. The puck dropped, and as soon as Dalton's stick hit the ice, I came underneath as heavy as I could and snapped the puck back.

The next face-off, I did the same thing. And then the one after that. After a while, Dalton knew what I was going to do on each face-off, and I still beat him. My new, not-so-secret move seemed to be working pretty well. Probably had something to do with getting Hall of Fame advice from one of the best players ever.

Making those sorts of minor improvements in my game was becoming more and more important as my minor midget season was wrapping up. I still wanted to be drafted into the OHL, but I was also seriously looking at playing in the NCAA, so my family and I visited a number of different schools and cities. My mom was particularly keen on me playing in the NCAA—she wanted me to get a good college education—and my dad agreed I should consider all of my options.

My mom and I took a couple of trips down to the University of Michigan. The first time we visited, we went down with my teammate and schoolmate Paul Rekai and his mom. We took a tour of the campus with one of the associate coaches of the hockey team, and then we got to watch the outdoor hockey game between the University of Michigan and Michigan State. It was called the Big Chill at the Big House. The whole campus was electric. People were tailgating and celebrating before the game even started, and I could feel the rumble of their chants in my chest as we entered the arena. I turned to my mom and said, "This is so cool." The game set a record for attendance at a hockey game, and I loved the atmosphere.

Not long after, I took a second trip down, this time with my dad. It was a more serious visit, but we still managed to catch another game between the two Michigan teams, each of which was captained by a future NHLer. Tory Krug led Michigan State, and Carl Hagelin was the captain of the University of Michigan. This time, the game was held inside at the Yost Ice Arena. After the game, my dad and I sat down with Red Berenson to talk about the University of Michigan program.

I still had to keep my options open, though, so we also went to visit the OHL teams in Windsor and London, Ontario. Each place looked better than the last, and as the list of places we visited grew longer, I kept asking myself, *Where can I play in front of the most fans possible?*

A lot was going to boil down to what happened during the OHL draft. The draft is done online, so on May 7, 2011, I was sitting at the kitchen table in my mom's house, streaming the draft live on my computer. I watched as my friends' names appeared—Darnell Nurse, then Jordan Subban. I was still watching when my phone rang.

"Is this Max?" the voice asked.

"Yes," I said distractedly, still staring at my computer screen.

"Congratulations," the person said. "I'm calling on behalf of the Kingston Frontenacs. We've just selected you as our first overall pick. We can't wait to have you join the team."

Sure enough, as the stream caught up, I saw it in writing: the Frontenacs had drafted me eighth overall.

My first reaction was a mixture of surprise and disappointment. I hadn't visited Kingston, so I couldn't create the same picture in my mind of me and my teammates in front of a roaring crowd as I had in the other places I'd been to. Before the draft, many teams had spoken to my parents and asked questions about my health. The organizations that had taken the time to call wanted to make sure they understood the challenges I faced and that they were comfortable with everything. The Kingston organization hadn't done that, though, so I worried that they didn't realize just what kinds of issues I dealt with daily. Were they going to be able to support me so that I could continue to succeed and make it to the NHL?

I called my dad, who helped calm me down. "Don't worry, Max," he said. "Everything is going to work out."

It was what I needed to hear, and I trusted my dad that everything would be fine. In the meantime, I looked into my other option of playing in the NCAA more seriously. I even went down to visit a USHL team, which would have been my segue from minor hockey to the NCAA.

Things did end up working out. At the end of August, I got another call, this time from the London Knights. I'd been traded!

When I heard the news, my heart skipped a beat. The Knights had been one of my top picks of places to play, and they had an amazing history. More important, I knew they had experience dealing with type 1 diabetes—they already had a player with diabetes on the team.

While I was excited to be going to the OHL to play for the London Knights, the fact remained that it wouldn't be an easy road ahead. I was confident in my abilities to play hockey at that level. But I had no idea whether or not I could control my diabetes and still play at the high level that I was used to.

Before I figured that out, though, I had a more pressing issue: I was about to move away from home. I knew how much I relied on my family, and to move away from them was to move away from the only support network I'd ever known. It wasn't going to be easy.

5

TRUST YOUR TEAM

My parents were a little stressed about the idea of me moving away from home. It wasn't that they thought I couldn't handle playing in the OHL. They were worried for my health. I understood where they were coming from. This would be the first time I didn't have the usual team who'd always kept me healthy—my parents, my sisters, our neighbors, the doctors at SickKids—immediately at hand.

As I packed up the car for the move, I could tell my parents were nervous. My dad looked like he hadn't slept in days, and he couldn't sit still. My mom was calmer on the surface, but I could tell she was thinking about the move.

"Are you worried?" I asked her on the drive to London.

"Of course I am," she said with a smile. She was always open about things with me. "But I know you'll make the right decisions. And you've worked hard to get here, and I'm excited to see what this next chapter brings for you."

Fortunately, all of our fears ended the moment that we met my amazing billet family in London. Gail and Scott Tooke were standing outside their house the moment we got there, and Gail greeted us with the warmest smile the moment we arrived.

"Max, it's so nice to meet you," Gail exclaimed, gathering me into a hug as I stepped out of the car. She turned to my parents. "Don't worry; we're going to take good care of him. We know exactly what's needed."

She meant that literally: Gail and Scott's son Noah—my billet brother—also had type 1 diabetes. Not only that, but they already had another billet who also played on the team, Jared Knight, living with them, and he had diabetes, too. When my parents learned that, I could see the weight lift off their shoulders. Suddenly living away from home didn't seem so intimidating. My parents were confident that Gail and Scott would know what to do if something ever happened to me.

When I moved in with the Tookes, it was the first time I'd really been around other people with diabetes around the clock. But although we all shared the same disease, we each had wildly different needs. I was dealing with my celiac diagnosis on top of my diabetes. Noah had a thyroid condition he had to manage. And Jared had only recently discovered his diabetes diagnosis.

Noah had been diagnosed at five years old, so he'd lived with his diabetes most of his life. Jared, though, was only diagnosed when he was eighteen. I fell between the two of them, which meant that each of us was at a different emotional stage in our diabetes management.

Although Noah was the youngest of the three of us, he was the one who taught us the most about the disease in our first few months together. I was still eating everything in sight and carrying juice boxes around with me everywhere—the empty juice boxes all over the house used to drive Gail crazy. Jared was new to managing his disease, so he was still trying to figure out what exactly his body needed.

Late one night, all three of us were starting to go low. We were hanging out in the kitchen, drinking one juice box after another, looking for something to eat.

"How about peanut butter?" Jared asked.

Noah and I looked at each other. "Jared," Noah said, "peanut butter's not a carb."

"What do you mean?" Jared asked, a spoonful of peanut butter already in his mouth. Noah and I understood—when you're low, you're not thinking clearly.

"I mean, eating a bunch of peanut butter isn't going to help bring up your blood sugar levels," Noah said, starting to laugh. His laughter was infectious, and whether it was the sight of Jared shoveling back spoonful after spoonful of peanut butter or just the fact that we all had low blood sugar levels, the three of us started laughing uncontrollably.

I had a ton of fun staying with the Tookes. They were a hilarious family, constantly playing pranks on one another, and it wasn't long until I was caught up in them.

Gail's husband Scott would make a protein shake for everyone in the mornings. One time, I asked Scott if we could make a "special shake" for Jared Knight. I raided the fridge, grabbed everything you could think of—mustard, ketchup, pickle juice—and poured a little of each into Jared's shake. Scott served the drinks like usual, and I said to Jared, "Knighter—this is one of the best shakes out there." He took the glass and, sure enough, he downed the whole thing.

We started laughing our heads off after he finished it, but Jared just looked at us questioningly. "What's so funny?" he asked. "That was pretty good."

The Tookes' kitchen had one of those spray handles you use in your sink to rinse your dishes—the kind where, when you press a button on the handle, the water stops coming out of the tap and starts spraying out of the spray nozzle. One night, Jared and I taped down the spray mechanism with Scotch tape so that whoever turned on the tap to fill the sink would get sprayed.

When dinner was done, Gail got up to start doing the dishes. Jared and I exchanged a look and tried to keep ourselves from laughing too early and spoiling the joke. Poor Gail—she turned on the tap and the nozzle sprayed water right in her face. After she got over her shock, Gail was howling with laughter like the rest of us.

Life in London was a nice change of pace from Toronto. I was in my last year of high school, and my parents were adamant that I finish my education, so I stuck it out in school. But I got some flashes of that carefree living that I hadn't had in a long time.

A lot of those fun moments were with Jared Knight at my side. Jared was like an older brother to me, and I followed him around everywhere. When he and I hung out, though, we didn't exactly make the brightest decisions. A lot of times, we were straight-up out to lunch.

One day we decided to try dying our facial hair. The only problem was that neither of us had much facial hair to begin with. I had a bit of peach fuzz, and Jared didn't have much more, but we spread the jet black dye across our faces, trying to color whatever hair I had. I started from my ears, went down my neck, and up to my cheekbones—it looked like I had a thick black beard of ink. Jared only put a little bit around his face, but he still looked like he had a black goatee.

We went downstairs to show Gail and Scott. They both looked at us like we were from another planet

"I want it to be darker," I said.

"Be careful with that stuff," Gail said.

Jared and I went back upstairs. After a few minutes, he turned to me and asked, "Do you feel it burning?"

"I thought it was just me!" I said.

"My face is on fire," he said.

"Let's see who can keep it on longer," I suggested.

Jared didn't last long. "I can't take this anymore," he said.

We both started to rinse the ink off. When I looked up from the sink to dry my face, I was horrified to realize that my face was still black. I tried not to panic, but then Jared picked up the box.

"Oh, no," he said. "We were only supposed to keep it on for five minutes. I don't know how you're going to go to school looking like that."

Jared and I went running back downstairs.

"We need some help," I said.

"Gail, what are we going to do?" Jared asked.

"Come here," she said. She mixed together some dish soap and rubbing alcohol with water, and she started scrubbing my face with a brush. She kept trying to wash off the ink, but even with her help, the dye just wouldn't come out. The three of us were laughing hysterically as she kept washing and scrubbing.

The next day, I went to school and my face was so raw, it was beet red. I must have walked around for another three days with some bits of dye still stuck in my skin.

You'd think I would learn from that, but there were countless incidents like that where Jared and I weren't the brightest duo. That being said, Gail and Scott were always there to make sure we didn't fall too far out of line.

School might not have kept me all that captivated, but playing hockey was something totally different. The second I pulled on a Knights jersey, I felt like I was home.

I will never forget my first time walking into the arena in London. The moment I entered through the doors, one of the older guys on the team, Colin Martin, called me over.

"Welcome to the Knights, Max," he said. I just smiled as I shook his hand—I was excited that he even knew my name!

Colin started showing me around the rink and dressing room and where everything was. It was all a blur—I couldn't believe I was really there. At one point, Colin caught me looking up at the banners in the rafters with a goofy grin on my face. He stopped, looked at me, and said, "It goes by fast, kid."

I heard the same thing from four or five other older players that same day. I tried to listen to what they were saying, but it was hard. I'd just arrived—I had tons of time, right? Plus, there was a lot to learn about my new team, and that was just on the ice. Off of it, I was struggling to get my health in order.

Being a sixteen-year-old kid with diabetes in the OHL wasn't easy, but being a celiac wasn't a walk in the park, either. My rookie year with the Knights was probably my most frustrating time as someone with celiac disease.

Like any teenager, I was constantly forgetting things when I packed for a road trip. Of course, I would always remember my iPad and headphones. But the important things—a snack for the bus ride or juice boxes—seemed to slip through the cracks more often than not. It wasn't a big deal when we were playing a team nearby, but some teams were hours away. When you are playing junior hockey, you can spend a lot of time on a bus.

Each trip, we would inevitably stop at a Tim Hortons, which was fine for my teammates. They could just run in and grab a sandwich or whatever snack they wanted. But for a long time, all I could order from Tim's was hot chocolate. I got really excited when they started offering strawberry-banana smoothies. Before that, though, if I forgot my gluten-free snacks, I would just be left sitting on the bus, sour and hungry.

Every time it happened, I would be so mad at myself for forgetting and putting myself in that situation. I would swear that I'd be better the next trip. But I kept doing it! I blamed my personality—I was so in the moment that if I was talking to someone, I would completely forget whatever I was supposed to be doing.

It took until the halfway point of that first season with the Knights for me to finally realize that I needed to take my nutrition more seriously and pack some food. Making sure I had something to eat on the bus had to take priority over hanging out at home an extra ten minutes or talking to the guys in the dressing room. I had to be more disciplined to leave that conversation and go get some food that I knew was safe to eat on the trip.

The list of foods that were safe for me wasn't long. Sometimes my billet mom Gail would make me chicken and rice. I would bring that, or a Tupperware container with gluten-free pasta in a red sauce. I was happiest when we pulled into one of those big ONroute highway stops because they had a bunch of good options—yogurt and nuts—that I could eat. Whenever we stopped at the ONroutes, I was the guy coming back to the team bus with $40 worth of healthy snacks. My teammates would all be holding bagels and staring at me with looks that said, *What the hell are you doing?*

In London, there was a big market—called Covent Garden Market—right across from the arena. I discovered this one restaurant in the Market that served chicken souvlaki with rice, Greek salad, and a little tzatziki. It was gluten-free, and I got it almost every single day I was in London. There was also a salad bar that I went to when I needed to change things up.

I was a big believer in routine. Once I found something that worked, I kept eating it. I knew where to go and what was safe. With both my diabetes and my celiac, if I didn't prepare for what was ahead of me or if I let my guard down, I'd be playing catch-up all day long. I knew the pattern—one screwup leads to another, and just like that, you're behind the eight ball, chasing your blood sugar. That was never a good place to be for any person with diabetes, let alone a semi-professional athlete.

If you are not calm, collected, and understanding your physical situation, you can run into trouble. You can't just go with the flow. I hated that—I always wanted to be the guy who could just roll with things. Finding a way to balance what my mind wanted and what my body needed took some practice.

One thing I found helped was music. Hockey was always number one in my life, but music was never far behind. It was my escape— the right song could take me to a good moment down memory lane in just a few bars. My music selection was inspired by the people around me, so my song choices were never consistent. I might have a whole bunch of Top 40 hits, followed by EDM, followed by hip-hop, followed by classic rock, followed by country. One of the hardest jobs on a hockey team that no one tells you about is being the team DJ, which I was. I took pride in catering to all of my teammates' needs when it came to music.

One of our rookie duties was bringing movies for bus trips. Usually, we'd stick to new releases, but you could never go wrong with one of the classics. I would howl along with the other guys when they put on *Caddyshack* or *Happy Gilmore*. The time I spent on those bus trips with my teammates were some of my most treasured moments from my junior career.

I loved being on the road. It was rare for us to stay overnight in a hotel. But whenever we did during my rookie year, my room-mate was Bo Horvat. Bo and I had been friends ever since we played against each other as kids. We'd had a rivalry on the ice, but it had been a respectful one, and we'd gotten along well when we talked after the games. Bo was the perfect roommate. He was like Jonathan Toews—he was Mr. Serious, always humble and hardworking. He'd had the same haircut since he was nine years old. He was incredibly responsible, too, which was probably why Bo was the one the coaches asked to partner up with me and make sure I was taking care of my diabetes on the road.

Every night before we went to sleep, Bo would look at me and ask, "Are you all good?"

"Yes," I'd say.

"All right, good night, buddy," he'd say, before rolling over and turning the lights out.

There's no self-help book about how to deal with diabetes, so I was glad to have such a close friend watching my back. There was so much to learn and experience that first year with the Knights, and I didn't have a playbook for how to handle every situation. Sometimes the only things I could do were listen to the voice inside my head and trust the guys on either side of me.

Early into the season with the London Knights, the older players held a rookie initiation. It wasn't that bad and there was nothing offside—they don't haze rookies like the old days anymore, thank goodness. It was basically just a party to welcome the new players to the team. That isn't to say I didn't have some anxiety about that night.

I was so nervous about our rookie party because I was going into a foreign situation with alcohol involved, and I wasn't totally sure of how the alcohol would affect my blood sugar levels. That was what gave me anxiety about the night. I wanted to have fun with my teammates and bond with them, and I wanted to enjoy the experience. But my parents had always told me that with my disease, I had to be extra careful if I was going to drink. They didn't approve of me drinking, but they wanted me to be prepared if I ever found myself in that situation.

I was also nervous because I didn't want the boys to be mad at me if I wasn't participating. It turned out I had nothing to fear. Jared Knight was one of our best players—he'd already been drafted into the NHL—and he'd earned a lot of respect among the team. Early into the night, he'd looked at me and said, "You don't have to do anything. If anyone asks you to do something you don't want to, just stick by my side." He filled in our captain at the time, Jarred Tinordi, and a couple of other teammates, Scott Harrington and Michael Houser, and they all agreed to keep an eye out for me.

I made it through the night without any problems, and later Jared ended up being the one who showed me how to have a couple of drinks now and then, but just be smart about it.

That kind of support from my teammates meant the world to me. Scott Harrington was two years older than me, and he and I ended up spending a lot of hours together driving to practices and games during my time with the Knights. Scott, or "Harry," as he was known, was an assistant captain by the time I joined the Knights, and he did a good job of showing me the ropes. I couldn't believe how welcoming and considerate all of the guys were at every step. I was thankful for it, as it made my rookie year even smoother than I had expected.

What I didn't find out until well after the rookie party was that, before the season had started, my dad had also pulled Jared and some of the older guys aside. He'd told them to watch out for me and make sure I was taking care of my diabetes.

When one of the older guys let that slip, I saw red. I called my dad right away.

"You shouldn't have got involved," I yelled into the phone.

"Your mom and I are just watching out for you. We don't want anything bad to happen to you."

"I can handle myself," I shouted as I hung up.

Even to this day, if my dad knows I'm heading somewhere for the first time, he'll try to call ahead or send word so that whoever I'm meeting knows about my diabetes.

When I eventually cooled down, I was able to see that my dad was just doing what any parent would. My parents had taught me how to be more mature than most kids my age. But that didn't change the fact that I was still their kid. I was trying to carve out my own space as an adult, but I knew they'd never stop looking out for me.

The closer we got to the playoffs in my first year, the more thankful I was for the support of my family and teammates. My first year of playing junior hockey had felt like the longest season ever. I had never played that much hockey before. Every day was fun, and we were playing in front of nine thousand fans at every home game. The whole season was a blur, and although those words from the seniors—"It goes by fast"—sometimes echoed in my head, the season felt like it was never going to end.

Once the playoffs started, we were all laser-focused on every single game. The older guys in the dressing room set the tone. Bo Horvat and I sat on either side of Austin Watson. It was an unusual setup—typically, the older, more experienced guys sit together on an island in the middle of the room, and the farther away you are from them, the less experienced you are. But when Austin showed up halfway through the season after a trade, he picked the stall between Bo and me, two of the youngest guys on the team.

My first impression of the older veterans was that they didn't mess around; hockey wasn't just a game to them. I took note. I was still making small mistakes, on and off the ice. But seeing the way those guys carried themselves and prepared, I was starting to realize just what it meant to be a pro.

For the first couple of rounds in the playoffs, we were pounding the opposing teams. We swept two of our three series—it seemed like nobody could stop us. We rolled through the competition and into the finals, where we beat the Niagara IceDogs to win the 2012 OHL Championship.

The victory was amazing, but we had our sights on a bigger goal: the Memorial Cup, given to the overall champion of the Canadian Hockey League. The champions of each of the three junior leagues—the Ontario Hockey League, the Quebec Major Junior Hockey League, and the Western Hockey League—and a host team all face off for the chance to be called the best junior team in the country.

At this point, the season was wearing me down. My diabetes made every day a struggle, but my focus on each game was so intense that I knew it would be fine.

The Memorial Cup tournament started well. We won two of our three round robin games, so we went directly to the championship, where we faced the Shawinigan Cataractes. It was a close game as we battled back and forth. We took the lead in the first period, but Shawinigan tied it up in the second. Neither of us could pull ahead after that, so the game went to overtime. With only a couple of minutes left in the extra frame, Shawinigan managed to work the puck in front of our net, where they scored to win the tournament.

We were devastated. In the dressing room after the game, I was shocked to see that guys were crying. To that point, I had viewed the older guys on the team as veterans who were so tough, it was almost like they were made of stone. I thought of our captain, Jarred Tinordi, as though he were a thirty-year-old man. To see those older players in tears after losing let me know just how much that game meant to all of us.

As a team, it was tough to lose that way. That had been our chance to win it all, and now we would have to start all over again. Sitting there, my sweaty gear still stuck to my body, my mind flashed back to a road trip to Sudbury we'd taken in February. The weekend had been exhausting. It was a six-hour drive one way, and all weekend it had been absolutely freezing. My mind fixated on the memory of all of us sitting around tables in a fast-food restaurant, eating the same bad food, each wearing the same team tracksuit, trying to keep our spirits and energy up to power through and get home.

I couldn't get that image out of my head. All the sacrifice and dedication we'd shown that year, only to lose our final game in overtime. I was so drained that it was hard to imagine how we could do it all over again. But as I looked around the room and saw the guys I'd battled beside for months, I told myself, *We'll be back.*

It helped that I didn't have time to dwell on our loss. There was more hockey to come, even before the next season began. In August 2012, I took part in the Ivan Hlinka Tournament, an annual international hockey tournament featuring the best under-eighteen-year-old hockey players from the countries invited.

The tournament took place just before I was supposed to arrive in London for my second training camp with the Knights. The timing didn't worry me, but something else did—this would be the first time I traveled overseas since I'd been diagnosed with diabetes.

The tournament was held in Břeclav, Czech Republic, and Piešťany, Slovakia, that year. It was my first time playing for Team Canada, and when I was handed my jersey, I traced the maple leaf on the front in wonder. *Team Ontario feels a long way away*, I thought. I was both immensely proud and nervous at the same time. Proud, because the tournament was a sign that I was entering a professional atmosphere, and I wanted to represent our country well. Nervous, because I didn't want my diabetes to stress anyone out or cause me to make mistakes.

The team officials were clearly on edge, too. When I got to the hotel cafeteria for my first meal, a team trainer came running up to me.

"Max, I've prepared a list of the foods that you shouldn't eat here," the trainer said.

"Thanks," I said with a smile. I'd already scouted ahead and knew exactly what was safe for me to eat, so I wasn't concerned.

"Just go grab a seat and I'll bring your food to you."

"You don't have to do that," I said. I was mortified—no one else on the team was being served their food.

"No, no, I insist."

I tried to argue, but it was no use, so I made my way over and sat down with the boys on the team. A few minutes later, the trainer dropped off a plate of food. On the edge of the plate was a name card with "Max" on it.

I could feel my face going red as I dug in. I knew that the trainer was just doing his job, but I didn't want the special attention. I would have preferred if I could have just quietly picked up my food on my own. I was grateful that none of my teammates said anything about it.

If it wasn't a trainer hovering over my shoulder, though, it was my dad. And if not my dad, my mom was there. Both of my parents had come over to watch me play, and they were everywhere that Team Canada was. My mom was so worried about me traveling that she had made laminated cards that described all of my medical conditions in three languages. She made me carry one, distributed them to the team trainers, and kept a stack on hand, just in case.

That was the peak of my no-one-else-can-tell-me-what-to-do phase. I felt that I had been dealing with my diabetes long enough that nobody else really knew what I was going through. If they didn't know what it was like to go low or go high, how could they tell me what to do? Did they not think that I knew how my own body worked? Did they think I couldn't take care of myself?

I should have been thankful for the help, because finding gluten-free foods in the Czech Republic and Slovakia wasn't easy. Telling someone that I had celiac disease didn't mean much, even to the guys on the team. I was in the middle of one of the most intense hockey tournaments I'd ever played in, and I was living off of salad, soup, and gluten-free peanut butter protein bars that the team trainers had packed.

The tournament was full of those sorts of eye-opening experiences. When it came down to it, though, we were there for one thing: hockey.

The night before we were supposed to play the Swedes, some members of the Swedish team snuck a video camera into our practice to film us. My dad, being the hockey-loving super-dad that he is, was watching our practice. He spotted the camera unattended and decided to head over and make sure it was shut off, one way or another.

As he walked over, the Team Canada coaches started firing pucks into the stands, trying to knock over the camera. The Swedish coaches heard the racket and didn't take that too well, and they were even less impressed when my dad finally picked up the camera and strolled off with it so that he could turn it off. But the guys on the team loved it—we were dying laughing as we cheered on the coaches.

The film didn't help the other teams—we were undefeated in the round robin, beat the Czech Republic in the semifinal, and then beat Finland 4–0 in the championship game. Nathan MacKinnon had a hat trick that night, and as we gathered around center ice with our gold medals, gluten-free food and medical cards were the last things on my mind.

The experience overseas set me up for my second year with the London Knights. Having seen how difficult it was to manage my diabetes without the right food available, I was much more thankful for the options I had at home.

One of the nicest things about the transition from minor midget hockey to the OHL was the quality of the facilities and the support staff. I don't think anyone knew better than the trainers what I had to go through on a day-to-day basis during the season.

In my second year with the Knights, I met with our new trainer, Doug Stacey. I sat down in Doug's office and talked him through everything about my diabetes. We tried to cover every single detail. He made a note of my prime blood sugar numbers, what to look for when I was off, and what foods I could and couldn't eat.

That was one of the hardest periods of my diabetes management. My body was changing—the way it responded to insulin and processed carbohydrates was different when I was seventeen than it had been when I was fourteen. And I knew it would be different again when I was twenty. And on top of that, I was trying to become a professional athlete, living away from home, trying to get drafted, and dealing with the rigorous schedule of junior hockey.

To manage all of that was a real team effort between Doug and me. When it came to our game-day routine, Doug and I had it down to a science. Doug would poke his head in and make sure I had measured my blood sugar levels an hour and a half before a game, then again before and after the warm-up. Once the game started, at every ten-minute mark, Doug would hand me my blood testing kit and I'd check again.

Even though we were constantly monitoring my blood sugar, Doug would still have all of our backup options in place on the bench, just in case there were any issues. He would keep a stock of insulin on the bench for me, along with extra drinks, some with sugar in them and some without. Whatever the situation, Doug was prepared.

Doug used to joke with me that he could always tell when my blood sugar was high because I would get super-aggressive on the ice. He'd see me charging into the corner all out, and when I got back to the bench, he'd quietly hand me one of the sugar-free drinks to help me balance out. If I was looking lethargic or wasn't back-checking as hard I could, he'd pass me one of the sugary sports drinks instead to get my numbers back up. And if I ever told him I needed something stronger, he would have glucose tablets on hand for an extra kick. Doug would never argue with me. He and I operated on trust, and we were in it together.

When you have type 1 diabetes as an athlete, you make a stronger connection to your trainer than most other players because you spend so much more time with them on a daily basis. There were some guys who never set foot in the training or medical rooms. But when you have type 1 diabetes, you get to know your trainer like he's family.

A few weeks later, I was having breakfast when I got a call from my dad.

"Max, make sure you're at practice today," he said.

"I'm at every practice, Dad."

"I know, but it's especially important today—Wayne Gretzky is coming by."

I laughed. "Sure, Dad."

"I'm serious. Make sure you're there."

I wasn't sure whether to believe my dad or not, so I didn't know how to respond. I couldn't believe that the Great One would show up at our practice for no reason. Surely he had more important things to get to?

A little while later, though, my dad called me back. He was serious about what he'd said earlier. It turned out Gretzky was in town for some other requirement, and—I'm not sure whose idea it was—my dad told me that a photographer was going to be there to take a picture of me and Gretzky. I still didn't know what that meant.

When I got off the ice from practice that day, sure enough, Wayne Gretzky was waiting outside our dressing room. I couldn't believe it!

I was still in my sweaty gear, but we spent some time just chatting together, which was priceless. At one point, a photographer did appear and took our photo. There's a famous picture that was taken years ago of Gordie Howe and Wayne Gretzky at a sports banquet. When Gretzky posed with Howe for the photo, Gordie took his stick and playfully hooked it around Wayne's neck. That day in London, I was sitting there in my practice jersey and Wayne had a suit on. Just before we took the photo, he grabbed one of my sticks and hooked it around me just like Gordie Howe did all those years ago.

I told myself that this year would be the big one for me. It was time for me to start playing hockey seriously and make it a full-time commitment. And that included staying on top of my diabetes with testing and insulin and diet.

I was starting to see my diabetes as a strength. It kept me focused and made me more responsible than I ever would have been if I didn't have it. It meant I was always focused on staying ready for the next shift, the next game, the next tournament. It gave me drive and purpose.

Up to that point, I'd never had any reason to see my diabetes as a weakness. It had never stopped me from doing the things other kids did, and nobody had ever chirped me about having diabetes. So when it happened that year, I was more surprised than anything. I had been jawing at an older player on another team, and we'd been pestering each other all night. Halfway through the game, he lined up beside our bench for a face-off, and one of my teammates said something pretty bad to him. The guy looked at the bench, but he seemed confused about who had taunted him. So he looked at me and said, "Hey, Domi, how's your diabetes doing, bud?"

It was the lamest chirp I'd ever heard. A split second passed, and then I started laughing along with the guys beside me.

"That's the best you can come up with?" I asked. The guy shut up after that.

On the ice, my second season was going well. But off the ice, things hit a rough patch. My first year had shown me how much freedom I had as a junior player. I didn't have any parents to answer to. That meant that my teammates and I could go out anywhere we wanted to, whenever we wanted to. It was unreal.

As a player, I was having success on the ice, which meant I was pretty much under the spotlight the whole time I was in London—the fans in that city love their team. As a team, we were setting records; at one point, we went on a twenty-four-game winning streak. The whole city was buzzing, and as a team, we were on a high. So, naturally, the bubble was about to burst.

It was February 2, 2013, and we were traveling from London to Owen Sound on a bitterly cold afternoon to go play the Attack. It was a long, dull drive, and on this particular night it was freezing cold and snowing.

All I wanted to do was curl up and go to sleep during the trip. So I put on a show on my iPad, and I was so exhausted that I was asleep halfway through it. When I woke up, I was in the back of an ambulance.

It was entirely my fault. When we'd left London, Doug, our trainer, had brought me my usual meal. He'd handed me the box, with "Max" written on the top.

"Thanks," I'd said without looking up from my phone. I'd put the meal on the seat beside me, and then I'd fallen asleep before I had a chance to eat it.

When the bus stopped at a Tim Hortons, I had still been resting. The boys knew I couldn't eat anything from Tim's, so they left me there while they grabbed some food. When the bus left the rest stop, I was still sleeping. It was only when we arrived at Owen Sound and everyone but me got off the bus that they realized something was wrong. A couple of guys had tried to wake me up.

"Max, are you all right? We need to go," they'd said as they shook my shoulder. But I was just lying there, absolutely soaked in sweat and staring straight ahead, completely still.

The boys had called over Doug, and he immediately gave me a shot of glucagon. Glucagon is another hormone produced by the pancreas. It stimulates the liver to release glucose into the blood, which increases blood sugar levels. A glucagon shot is a part of the low blood sugar emergency kit—the shot comes with several parts that have to be mixed together, so there are a few steps needed to prepare it when it's being given to a person who is having a severe low sugar reaction. It's basically an EpiPen for diabetes. A shot of glucagon can raise a person's blood sugar level quickly if its dangerously low, or hypoglycemic. In those cases, the blood sugar level is so low that you can lose consciousness, so the glucagon is incredibly important.

But the glucagon shot wasn't enough. Luckily, there was an ambulance at every OHL game and this one was sitting right next to our team bus, so the paramedics ran over.

They filled me in on everything as we drove to the hospital. I could barely recall what they were talking about—it felt like I had dreamed the past few hours.

"Do you know where you are, Max?" one of the paramedics asked me as they gave me a second shot of glucagon.

"Florida," I said groggily.

"Where?"

My head started to clear as the glucose hit my bloodstream. "Owen Sound," I said slowly. "I'm here to play hockey."

By the time we got to the hospital, I had recovered. When the doctors came in to check on me, I said, "I feel one hundred percent. I'm ready to go play."

Doug had come to the hospital with me, and he immediately shot down that idea.

"We already decided—you're sitting out the game for precautionary reasons," Doug said. "You gave us a good scare, Max. We're not taking any chances"

I finally managed to convince the doctors to let me go watch the last half of the game from the stands. Afterward, the guys came over to tell me their version of the events. They kept saying what a great job Doug had done, and most of them admitted they'd had no clue what to do. A lot of them were still shaken.

It was weird to see my teammates react that way. These were some big, tough hockey players, but they had never seen me or anyone else experience anything like that before.

"Thanks, guys," I said. "I really appreciate that you've all got my back. I'm sorry for putting you through that."

The worst part of the whole thing was that the team had to contact my billet family, and they would then have had to tell my mom and dad. I knew that was a phone call that would have made my parents feel sick. I hated making them worry, but they were just happy that I was okay and that everything turned out all right.

That was the only junior game that I missed because of my diabetes. I was so mad at myself. How in the world had I forgotten to eat? I'd made all these promises to myself and set these goals for making this my best year yet, and I'd let my guard down again.

Doug and I had a talk after we got back to London, and we both agreed that the scariest thing was how fast things could go sideways with this disease.

"Max, I'm glad you're okay," Doug said. "This can't happen again. We got lucky this time. Let's learn from this and grow from it."

Doug knew I wanted to play in the NHL. And he told it the way it was, even if it meant hitting a nerve and telling me something I didn't want to hear. But he also knew how to help me get back on track.

Around Easter in my second year, Doug invited me over to his house for dinner. When I got there, Doug introduced me to his six-year-old daughter, Delaney.

"Do you want to play the Easter egg hiding game?" she asked me immediately.

"Absolutely," I said. "How do you want to do it?"

"I'll hide Easter eggs around the house, and you look for them. Then we switch and I get to find them."

For the next two hours, I felt like a little kid. We went tearing around the house, pulling chocolate eggs out of drawers and from under furniture. Finally, Doug had to stop us so that we could all eat dinner.

Being in a welcoming home like Doug's on the holiday was fantastic, and it helped me to clear my head. I remained close with Doug's family, too—Delaney even changed her jersey number to 16.

With the incident on the bus behind me, I zeroed back in on my goal of being the best player and person I could. And it paid off. Our team kept getting better and better, and when the playoffs rolled around, we were crushing teams again, just like we had the year before.

We ended up facing a tough Barrie Colts team in the OHL finals and they had us on the ropes. We were down three games to one, and we looked to be finished.

Game six went to overtime. Barrie scored four straight goals in the third to force the extra frame. They were surging, and we dug deep to try to hold them off. A minute and a half into overtime, I fed a cross-ice pass over to Ryan Rupert, and he one-timed it past the

Barrie goalie for the winner. As I raced toward Ryan to celebrate, I didn't even feel like I was skating—I felt like I was flying. We'd pulled out a 5–4 win to force a seventh and deciding game. And even better, the game was going to be back in Budweiser Gardens, our home ice.

After we won in Barrie, our hope was rekindled. We had forced a game seven, and we had a chance to win an OHL championship on home ice.

The final game was neck-and-neck the whole way. Neither team was going down without a fight. Bo Horvat gave us a 1–0 lead in the first period, but Barrie tied it up shortly after that. We jumped ahead again in the second period, but with less than three minutes to play, the Colts tied the game.

You could feel the air go out of our bench for a moment after Barrie scored. But we never gave up. As the seconds ticked by and the prospect of overtime loomed, we threw everything we had at the Colts. Then, with just 0.1 second left on the clock, Bo did the unthinkable and buried the puck in the net before the clock ran out. The look on Bo's face as he threw his gloves in the air and raced toward our bench was priceless—I'd never seen him that excited before. The goal was reviewed, but when the dust settled, it was ruled a good goal. We'd won 3–2 to become OHL champions for the second year in a row. Our bench emptied and piled around each other in front of our net in a giant celebration. It was easily the loudest I'd ever heard the building.

It was just over a month before the NHL Entry Draft, and we were going back to the Memorial Cup. I thought back to the dressing room the year before and our overtime loss, and I smiled. *Told you we'd be back*, I thought. Unfortunately, our experience at the

2013 Memorial Cup was a step back from the year before. We won our first game, but then we lost our next two. The second one was particularly painful, as the Halifax Mooseheads blew us out 9–2.

We made it to the tiebreaker game, which we won, putting us through to the semifinals against the Portland Winterhawks. Halfway through the second period, I scored a power play goal to put us up 1–0. All we had to do was not let up and we'd be through to the finals again! But our run through the OHL playoffs had been emotionally and physically draining, and we didn't have any gas left in the tank. Portland came back with a fury that we couldn't match. Only a couple of minutes after I scored, they tied the game up, and they added another goal in the third period to win the game 2–1, ending our hopes of winning the championship.

I hated losing, and I hated even more that we'd gone all the way to the Memorial Cup two years in a row and lost both years. I told myself that there would be other opportunities, other tournaments, and other championships to win.

But, more than anything, I told myself to hold it together—there were bigger things on the way. After all, the NHL Combine and the NHL Entry Draft were only a few weeks away.

6

LEARN FROM FAILURE

Just before the end of my second year in London, I felt it was time for a change. So I did what every parent fears their kid will do: I decided to get a tattoo.

I had wanted one for a long time. I'd always felt they were a cool statement, and when I found out that my buddy Jared had a tattoo, I thought they were even cooler. My parents knew it was inevitable. My mom had just one rule.

"Make sure it's in reference to something significant in your life. Don't get something you'll regret."

It was good advice. What sort of image would I never get sick of? Finally, it came to me— I should pick something that related to my type 1 diabetes. After all, that was something I was going to be living with my entire life, and it was a big part of my life. There was no way my parents could get mad at me for that.

The chef at the Budweiser Gardens was named Kim, and she had full-sleeve tattoos. Kim and I were friends—she would prepare gluten-free meals for me, so we were always talking about my diet—and I told her I was thinking of getting a tattoo.

"What were you thinking of getting?" she asked.

"I want it to look like the medical alert bracelet. I always have to take off my bracelet for hockey, and I've already lost a few, so why not have the tattoo show the same symbol and then I won't need to wear a bracelet at all?" I said. The medical alert bracelet features the caduceus symbol—two snakes wrapped around a pole that is topped with a pair of wings. The symbol is associated with the Greek god Hermes, and it represents healing. My idea was to use that as the image for my tattoo, but I would also add the words "Type 1" to it.

She smiled. "I like it. You should go see the guy I use. His name's Sean. He's a big Knights fan—he'll help you out."

Sean agreed to see me, even though he had a yearlong waiting list at the time—a good sign that he knew what he was doing.

I reassured my mom that the tattoo would just be a little thing on my arm. But when Sean stenciled it out before starting, my first thought was, *Whoa, that's pretty big.*

I was a bit nervous, but I trusted Sean's judgment, and when he was finished, it looked fantastic. Now I had a daily reminder of the disease I had to respect and manage every day of my life. It was right there for everyone to see: I had type 1 diabetes.

The tattoo was the first step in my transformation during that time. The second was the NHL Entry Draft. The draft had been marked on my calendar for months, if not years.

But before putting on my best suit to attend the draft, I would have to attend the annual NHL Scouting Combine. The combine was the same thing every year—an event spread out over a few days where all the teams in the NHL physically and mentally measured all of the players in that year's draft class. But for each individual player, it was more than just a standard test. It was our moment to stand out and make an impression, for better or for worse.

I was nervous for the physical tests. I wasn't injured, but I was completely burned out. For two years in a row, we'd gone all the way to the Memorial Cup, and between that and the international competitions I'd played in, the games had added up. I was worried that if I underperformed in the physical tests, it would hurt my chances in the draft. Luckily, my agent, Pat Brisson, was there to reassure me.

"There are other players who went deep in the playoffs and all the way to the Memorial Cup, just like you did. And they aren't doing the physical testing, either, so you don't have to do it if you don't want to. The scouts already know what you can do on the ice," he said. That was a relief to hear because I had pushed my body and was overdue for some rest.

One thing I couldn't miss, though, were the individual interviews with the NHL teams. They were an important part of the process. One of my first interviews was with the Boston Bruins. As I walked into the meeting room, I was a bit on edge. I could hear a buzzing in my ears, and my skin was warm to the touch. I tried telling myself I had no reason to be nervous, but I didn't want to mess up.

I sat at the head of a big boardroom table and looked around at a group of faces I'd never seen before.

"Hi, Max," said the head scout. "Thanks for meeting with us today. We wanted to start off with an easy question—what's your favorite animal?"

I froze. I was expecting questions about my workout habits or how I worked with a team. But my favorite animal? That was weird. I tried not to panic and blurted out the first thing that came to mind.

"I guess it'd be a dolphin," I said.

I watched the scouts glance down at their papers and try to hide their laughter. Suddenly it dawned on me—they didn't care what my favorite animal really was. It was a joke—considering the team's historical logo, there was only one answer to a room full of Boston Bruins staff.

"After a bear, of course," I added.

They were nice about it, and we moved on to the next question, but I couldn't help feeling liked I'd failed my first test.

The rest of the day went a little more smoothly. It was a long haul. I met with almost every single team in the league, with the exception of one or two. Some meetings were five minutes long, others went a little longer. It would have been easy to get frustrated at the fact that I basically had to regurgitate the same answers for every single interview. The teams had been following me and the other players on the ice for years, so they knew our abilities well by the point of the combine. The purpose of the meetings was to get to know us better as people. I wanted to be myself and be genuine, but it was challenging to figure out how to say the same thing over and over again. I just hoped I had made my best impression.

The hardest part, though, was that when it was all said and done, there was only one thing I could do: wait. It would be a few more weeks before the draft day in Newark, New Jersey, and all I could do before then was try to keep my mind off of the draft and everything it held for my future. Just that.

The less I thought about it, the faster the time went by. But that was hard because the draft entered my mind at some point every day! During the week leading up to the draft, time seemed to kaleidoscope in front me, and each hour felt like an eternity.

I spent the morning of the draft with my dad. We were getting ready in the apartment of a family friend, Nelson Peltz. My mind was buzzing, and I was checking my phone in case there were any last-minute developments.

I was in my own little world. One minute, my pulse would spike at a rumor on Twitter that the Toronto Maple Leafs might trade up to pick me. The next, I was flashing back to games in junior, second-guessing decisions and trying to remember if I had made mistakes in front of any of the scouts who had been watching me all year.

After a while, I looked up to give my eyes a break and noticed a fancy chair across the room. It was a big chair, and it had ornate wooden legs. For no good reason, that chair started to draw all of my attention, and I just sat there staring at it, lost in my thoughts. Suddenly a voice inside in my head yelled, *Snap out of it!* My mind was hazy, and I clumsily reached for my glucose meter, my blood tester, held it to my fingertip, and felt the familiar pinch of the needle as it drew a bit of blood. The readout on the device told me what I already knew: my blood sugar was low.

Luckily, we were prepared. My dad had made sure the apartment was loaded with every fruit and juice you could think of. Whenever I stayed in a hotel and my blood sugar went low, it took time to track down a snack or something to balance me out. But in the apartment, it was all right there at my fingertips in case anything happened.

It was only a short walk to the kitchen, but I moved unsteadily. Thankfully, I made it there without falling. Immediately after chugging some juice, I was feeling more like myself, and I was able to regroup after some downtime.

It was a good thing, too, because the day would test my patience and energy. The whole thing was a lot of hurry-up-and-wait. Hurry up to the hotel lobby, then wait for a bus to Newark. Hurry into the venue, and then wait for your seats.

I was nervous, but the excitement and happiness that I was feeling made the nerves a good thing—it helped balance me out. As we made our way into the arena, I made sure to check my blood sugar again, just in case. The stress and anticipation could easily have thrown my levels out of whack, which was the last thing I wanted on a day like that.

TSN had assigned a crew to follow me and a few other players around all day to put together a draft special. I thought it was a little embarrassing, so every time I looked at the camera guys, I pretended to not know who they were. For a guy who hates attention, having a camera crew follow me and my family all day was the last thing I wanted.

The crew was there on the trip to the arena. They were there when I was hanging with the other draftees in the lobby. They followed me right up to the moment when the Coyotes' GM, Don Maloney, called my name and I walked onstage and shook Gary Bettman's hand.

"Welcome to the NHL," Bettman said. Four words I'll never forget.

After I'd made my way offstage and gone through the photo lineup, I was immediately pulled aside for an interview with TSN. I was pumped—I couldn't wait to tell everyone how excited I was to have been drafted and how I was looking forward to taking the next step in my career. Then my dad showed up. It turned out the station wanted us to do the interview together. I was a little pissed. Inside, I was thinking, *Hey, I got drafted today, not you.* But my dad was great about it—anytime the host tried to ask him a question, he brought it back to my future, which I really appreciated. He was just a proud dad who wanted to talk about his son.

After the interview, I was thrown into a media scrum backstage with the rest of the drafted players. The first person I saw was my buddy Bo Horvat. I went over and gave him a big hug, saying, "Dude! Congrats!"

"I can't believe we're both wearing NHL jerseys," he said, his grin never leaving his face.

I couldn't stop smiling all afternoon, either. When my obligations were finally over and I was able to see my family, though, I was drained. I didn't want to talk to a single person, but people kept dropping by—Nick Kypreos stopped by to catch up, and then Ken Daneyko dropped by a little later. I was so thankful they'd taken the time to visit, but it was all I could do to keep myself from falling asleep.

I managed to get some food, which rebalanced my blood sugar levels and gave me some energy. It was a good thing, too, because I still had to meet with the Coyotes assistant coach, Jim Playfair. Jim came into the Phoenix Coyotes suite and chatted with my parents for a bit before delivering the real news.

"Max, we're going to be having a development camp in a few weeks," he said. "We're excited to have you there. I hope you like the heat."

It was the best news I'd had all day. Being drafted to the NHL was one thing, but there was always the chance I'd spend years in the minors waiting for my chance to start with the team. The development camp wasn't the same as making the team, but it was the next step. I couldn't wait for a chance to prove to the coaches that I had what it took to play in the big leagues.

When my obligations were finally over, I was able to meet up again with my mom and dad, and we headed back to the hotel. When we got there, my sisters and extended family were waiting, ready to celebrate. The day had taken so much out of me physically and emotionally that I just wanted to get some sleep. But I also wanted to savour the moment with my family, so I enjoyed every minute I could with them until I just couldn't stay awake any longer.

My mom walked with me to the elevator.

"I'm so proud of you, Max," she said. "You've worked so hard for this. It's everything you've ever wanted."

"I have you and Dad to thank for getting me here."

"You have yourself to thank for it. You've earned it. I can't wait to see what you'll do next. Congratulations, bud."

I crawled into bed, ready to collapse. The emotional roller coaster of the day, the lack of food, and the high-stress situations had me completely fried. Just before I went to sleep, I checked my phone. I had a ton of text messages from all of my friends who'd just been drafted. They were all out celebrating their big day with family and friends, having the time of their lives. But while their night was just heating up, I was out cold.

Two weeks after the draft, I found myself in the dry Arizona heat, standing outside an arena called the Ice Den. When I walked into the dressing room, I couldn't believe the sight of an NHL locker with my name on it. Even better, it was filled with a whole set of official NHL equipment. I was like a kid in a candy shop. My helmet, pants, and gloves—every piece had the NHL and Coyotes logos on it. As I laced up my skates for the first time, I felt like a pro.

The camp itself was fun and challenging at the same time. The point wasn't to figure out who was going to make the team—that would come in training camp later in the year. This was a chance for us younger players to become familiar with the organization, the facilities, the staff, and each other.

I'd finally recovered since our Memorial Cup run, so I was ready to get going. At least, I thought I was. I had been gradually easing back into training the past few weeks, but we skated our asses off in that camp. Each night, I had only enough energy to shuffle back to my hotel room and collapse into bed, wondering if I would be able to recover enough to stand out the next day. And each morning, I would haul myself out of bed and get ready to go all-out again.

The coaching staff knew how to balance things out, though. They wanted to see we could work hard, but they also wanted us to know that the Coyotes weren't just a team, they were a community. So they organized fun outings in the evenings for us to take part in. A couple of nights into the camp, the team even arranged to have me throw the first pitch at an Arizona Diamondbacks game.

I tested my blood sugar when I got to the park that night, and it was a little low. *It's just the nerves*, I told myself. My palms were so sweaty—something that I dealt with frequently as a person with type 1 diabetes—that I could barely hold on to a baseball. How was I going to throw it?

The other guys on the team had come to the game, and they were chirping me nonstop. "Remember not to bounce the ball," they said. "Don't throw it in the dirt."

"Excuse me," I said to one of the Diamondbacks staff. "Exactly how far is it from the mound to the plate?"

"It's a little over sixty feet," they said.

That was way farther than I'd thought. I was so scared I would mess up that I asked the team's backup catcher to come out so we could warm up my arm. We threw the ball back and forth underneath the stands for a while, and I gradually began to feel better.

But then we stepped onto the field. When I saw the distance for real, all I could think was, *Holy shit, that looks far!*

A PR rep from the team walked me out to the mound, and as

we crossed the outfield, the announcer read out my name and the crowd gave a cheer that made my stomach churn. The last thing I wanted was for my new team's fans' first impression of me to be that I couldn't even throw a ball. I leaned over to the PR rep beside me and asked, "I don't have to go all the way to the top of the mound, do I?"

All of the other rookies on the team were lined up along the first base line, watching me. I kept telling myself not to look at any of them, because they had all promised they'd do everything they could to make me laugh.

I picked a spot that I figured was close enough to the mound that it looked like a respectable distance but also where I knew I could make the throw. When I watched the video afterward, though, I saw that I was only ten steps away from home plate. I then proceeded to make the feeblest, most awkward throw to the catcher you could imagine. People watching it probably couldn't believe I was an athlete.

The catcher was nice about it. "All right, good job, man," he said as he jogged over and returned the ball to me.

My teammates waited until we were off the field to start laughing. "Dude, you were only a few steps away and you still lobbed it in there!" I laughed along with them. It looked like my baseball career wasn't going to start anytime soon.

The rest of the summer was a blur of camps of one sort or another. I went away for a week to the World Junior camp in August. Then, right after getting back from that, I had to leave for the Coyotes rookie training camp, which—if I made it—would be followed by the team's main training camp and then NHL exhibition games.

First, though, I had to earn a spot on the team. The training camp was a lot different from the development camp a few months prior.

That had been a guaranteed weeklong event for just the rookies. This time, I had no idea how long I would be there. If I made the team, I'd be living in Scottsdale full-time. But I could also be sent home after the first round of cuts.

At first I didn't know how to interact with the older guys on the team, which was odd for me. Thanks to my dad, I had basically grown up in an NHL dressing room. But I'd only ever been there as a visitor. Now I was there as an athlete, and I was stuck in the disbelief stage.

My roommate during camp was Jordan Schwartz. He was a young guy, but he'd been in the organization for a few years. He was veteran with the Coyotes' AHL affiliate team, and he knew the lay of the land. Jordan took me under his wing, and he introduced me to some of the older guys who were then playing in the AHL. We ended up hanging out together throughout the week. They took me and the younger players out to meals, showed us around town, and we played pickup games of volleyball to kill the time. It was kind of like being at summer camp.

Of course, at summer camp you're not competing against your cabin mates and you don't have an underlying risk of being sent home early. Trusting Jordan as my guide and distracting myself by hanging out with the other guys helped me from dwelling on those thoughts. Without those supports, I would have driven myself insane just sitting around the hotel every day, wondering whether I was about to be sent home.

But even when I was hanging out casually with the guys, I realized that playing hockey at that level was a job. There was a clear difference in mentality. The older guys were working so hard because they were trying to make a living. I was just a kid who was happy to be there. That sort of outlook is great for maintaining a positive attitude, but it doesn't get you far in the NHL. Every single second—whether it's in camp, in the dressing room, or on the ice—mattered. I quickly realized I needed more of an I-need-to-be-here mind-set if I was going to stick around.

I tried to bring that urgency to the rink. My line mates for our first intersquad games were Martin Hanzal and Radim Vrbata, two guys from the Coyotes' first line. When I saw my name on the whiteboard in the dressing room with Hanzal and Vrbata beside it, my first thought was, *Wow, I can't believe I get to play with these two guys*. I knew it was a huge opportunity, and a great test.

Hanzal and Vrbata could tell I was nervous. As we walked down the hallway, Hanzal gave me a little whack with his stick on the shin pads. "Relax," he said. "Have some fun out there. Go be you."

I took his advice to heart, and it seemed to pay off when the coaching staff kept me around to the end of camp. I was thrilled—I was going to be playing in my first NHL games! They might have been preseason games, but I didn't care. I was going to make my big league debut, and I couldn't be happier. I immediately called my parents. "I'm going to be playing in my first NHL preseason game tomorrow!" I told them.

"That's incredible news, Max!" my mom said. "We're so proud of you."

My dad was quick to tell me he would be there. I was pumped—to have him in the crowd was special to me.

I wish I could say that the beginning of my NHL career was like something out of a Hollywood movie. Unfortunately, it wasn't quite the movie I'd imagined

It was September 15, 2013. We were playing the Los Angeles Kings that night. I tried to keep calm as I got ready for the game.

Because of my nerves, my blood sugar had been low all day, so I was chugging apple juice before the game. I basically had a juice box glued to my hand while I got dressed, during warm-ups, all the way through the national anthem.

The juice solved one problem—it kept my blood sugar levels up. But it created another issue. I was bloated from all the liquid in my stomach, so skating at top speed got harder each shift. And the more I pushed myself, the more upset my stomach became. There's a lot of acid in apple juice—I didn't have a chance.

Partway through the second period, I got off the ice, and our head coach, Dave Tippett, tapped me on the shoulder, signaling he was double-shifting me. I jumped over the boards, and all of a sudden the nausea hit me like a brick wall. I took a deep breath and tried to swallow it down as I lined up for a face-off. One of the Kings defensemen was waiting for the puck drop when he caught my eye and asked, "Are you okay, man?" I could feel the sweat pouring off of my face—way more than there should have been.

"I'm fine," I managed to blurt out before tapping down my stick for the draw.

The Kings won the face-off, and their defenseman started skating up the ice. He was my guy to cover, and I started racing after him. Then I felt my stomach bubble up. I looked to our bench, and I knew it was too far away. *I'll never make it*, I thought. I immediately covered my mouth with my glove, and puked all of the juice I'd been drinking into it as I skated to the bench. There had to be a few liters of juice in my system at least. Thankfully, the Kings had turned the puck over and the play was going back toward their end. I dumped the vomit out of my glove and onto the ice, hoping nobody noticed, and hopped over the boards.

When I sat down, I immediately started puking everywhere. My head was between my knees, and the whole time I was thinking that if this game was in Toronto, I would already be all over YouTube.

All the coaches and all my teammates were immediately concerned. "Max, are you okay?" asked our trainer. "What's wrong?" They thought it was something serious caused by my diabetes. I waved them off and tried to downplay it, but I was embarrassed and ashamed of what had happened.

I made it through the rest of the game without any incident, but later one of our trainers expressed doubt about whether I would be able to withstand play in the NHL. I couldn't blame him. I'd been able to get away with stuff like that in junior—sometimes guys could coast during a shift and still be effective if they got a lucky break. But the NHL was a whole different level. You couldn't take a single second off. I wasn't going to be able to coast my way through anything.

I'd seen throughout training camp that it would take so much more than just talent to make it in the NHL: a heck of a lot more. And I knew I still had a long way to go. Physically, I was going to have to step up. But I would also have to be stronger mentally. I realized that getting even better at managing my diabetes would be the difference. Just working on hockey wasn't going to be good enough; I needed to work on my discipline, too.

I would have lots of time to do that. At the end of the preseason, our GM, Don Maloney, broke the news to me—I was being cut from the team that year and sent back to the OHL. I hadn't seen it coming, but I tried to be positive.

"You had a great camp," Don said.

"Thanks," I replied.

"You just have to get a year older and continue to get stronger," he said.

I thanked Don and Steve for the opportunity and promised I'd be back. But inside, I was confused and upset by Don's answer. What did getting older have to do with anything? I just wanted someone to tell me why I wasn't making the team, so I could go work on that.

I liked to consider myself mature beyond my years. But my reaction to the news told a different story. I hadn't ever experienced major failure like that before, and I didn't handle it like an adult should. I flew back to London right away to get to the next Knights game. I was sitting in the middle seat of the plane, sporting a big black eye courtesy of a high stick from San Jose's Scott Hannan. I was feeling so sorry for myself that, when I started to go low, I just kept wallowing in how bad I felt. I took care of my low, but I wasn't interested in being positive or even in the exact level of my blood sugar, for that matter.

I made it back in time for the game against Guelph, but I carried my foul mood with me—I got suspended in the first period for throwing an elbow to the head of Brock McGinn. McGinn later admitted to me that he sold the elbow to make it look worse than it was. Not that it mattered—that elbow I threw was a really dirty hockey play, and I deserved to be suspended.

You'd think that a moment like that would be a wake-up call. It should have been, but I didn't care after I got the news. My attitude was, *I'm too good for this league*—I felt like it was a waste of time to be back with the Knights. I was bitter and petty, constantly playing the blame game. I remember watching Coyotes games and thinking that I should be there. But, with time, I was able to see that I did have a lot to learn and a long way to go.

In December 2013, Team Canada announced its roster for the World Juniors. The same way that I'd expected I would make the Coyotes, I assumed I had a good chance of making Team Canada.

I mistook the few NHL preseason games I'd played for invaluable experience, and I was naïve enough to think that I had cemented a spot on Team Canada. I was so caught up in thinking that I should be in the NHL that I'd lost track of what was important—trying to get better on a day-by-day basis in London and earn a spot on Team Canada.

The day of the announcement, I had a weird feeling in the pit of my stomach. A voice in the back of my head kept repeating, *I didn't make this team.* I couldn't explain it. I had never had a defeated thought like that before in my life, and I'd never been cut from a team before the Coyotes. But I couldn't get that voice out of my head.

I was at the rink getting ready for a Knights practice when I got the call from Scott Salmon at Hockey Canada. He was kind, but he got right to the point—I wouldn't be playing for Team Canada that year.

My brain shut off when I heard that. I thanked him for the opportunity and wished him luck. After we hung up, I went through practice, and then I went to work out with my trainer.

I was in the gym for my warm-up, trying to act like what had just happened didn't matter. I felt very emotional, but I tried to downplay what a big deal it was for me. Everything felt out of my power. I felt so shitty, like I couldn't do anything to make a difference. What was the point in pushing so hard if I kept failing? It was easily the biggest sense of disappointment I had ever felt in my hockey career.

After the news was made public, I checked out who was on the roster. Bo had made it, and I was so happy for him. And another one of our teammates, Josh Anderson, would be going, too, which was fantastic. I was excited for both of them, and I wanted them to win. But knowing that I wouldn't get to be there beside them just doubled my disappointment.

The first person I called was my dad. I broke the news to him.

"Don't worry about it," he said. "Focus on winning another championship with the Knights. That's all you can control at this point."

The rest of my family called, along with my agent, Pat Brisson, and other friends. I tried to listen to the comforting words that everyone shared, but none of it made me feel any better.

But then I got a call from Mark Hunter, the general manager of the Knights. He told me he thought I should be at the tournament, but that we would make the best of the situation, and that we would do something special in London.

Mark's words struck a chord. After our call, I looked at myself in the mirror, knowing that I had to change my ways. It was time to collect myself and grow up—I had no one to blame but myself. If I was going to succeed or fail, it was all up to me and my play on the ice. The ball was in my court; it always had been.

Something clicked, and I went on a tear over the rest of the season—I ended up with thirty-four goals and ninety-three points in sixty-one games that year. More important, I didn't have any more diabetic incidents that affected my play throughout that time. As summer approached, I felt stronger and more assured every single day. I knew what I could do if I kept my body healthy and my mind in the right place.

I didn't know if all of that would be good enough to play in the NHL the next season. But at least I was one step closer to my dream. After everything that had happened that year, that was a start.

7

WILLPOWER IS A SUPERPOWER

I went back to Coyotes training camp for the second time in September 2014. What a difference a year made. At my first NHL training camp the previous year, I had been in awe of everything that was going on. My anxiety had been through the roof, and the practices had been like nothing I'd ever experienced.

When I showed up for my second camp, I didn't have quite the same deer-stuck-in-the-headlights feeling. I had traveled with the guys on the team, I had practiced with the boys, and I knew the coaches a little bit better. In some small way, I felt like I belonged a bit more than I had the first time around. It was a refreshing feeling.

My second year was still a challenge, but not even close to what I had gone through during my first camp. I did everything I could to make things easier on myself, too. Our first trip that camp, I sat down and made myself a checklist of what I needed to pack. Some of the items were no-brainers—toothbrush, deodorant, clothes. But others were things that no other player would pack—gluten-free snacks, insulin, test strips, batteries for my glucose meter. The guys on the team teased me for overpacking, but I found the exercise calmed me down. I knew I was prepared and that I had everything I could possibly need on the road if something went wrong.

The preparation seemed to help, as I played really well through-out camp and felt I was making an impact during our preseason games. I had put the previous year behind me. I really felt that I could have played in the NHL that year. But the Coyotes felt differently—they sent me back to London a second time, even earlier into camp than they had the year before.

The day that I was packing up to leave, our general manager, Don Maloney, came by to wish good luck to me and the other guys leaving camp.

"Don," I said as we shook hands, "last year I was told I had to get a year older and a year stronger. I did that. Can I ask, then, why I'm going back to London?"

Don smiled. "Another year of getting stronger won't hurt," he said. "I've seen young players in the past be thrown into the pros too early—it's not usually a good thing for them. When you come into the league, I want you to stay in the league."

I appreciated Don's insight, even if I didn't fully agree. But there was one difference that year, compared to the year before. Our head coach, Dave Tippett, pulled me aside just before I left.

"You can take being sent down however you want," he told me. "But if you want to be in the NHL next year, you can't afford to feel bad for yourself. You can't afford to mope around and think you're too good for the OHL. The window to make this team is small for everyone. We see you as being a big piece of this team. My challenge to you is to treat every day in London this year as if you're in the NHL. Practice habits, eating right, preparation. Do it all like a pro, and become a leader."

I've always been competitive, so if someone gives me a challenge, I take it. Dave Tippett gave me a challenge for that last year in Lon-don, and I embraced it.

Because of that, I had a much better attitude heading back to the OHL that year. I didn't see junior as punishment for not making the Coyotes roster; instead, I took it as an opportunity. I was determined to dominate junior hockey right away, so as soon as I got back I went right to work. I wanted to prove to everyone—my teammates, the Coyotes coaches, the Team Canada management—that I could be the mature player they wanted me to be. I hadn't forgotten being cut from the Team Canada World Junior team the year before. The tournament was going to be held jointly in Montreal and Toronto that year, and I wanted to be on the ice for it.

I played the best hockey of my life in the first few months after the Coyotes camp. I started to incorporate the lessons I'd learned and observed at the NHL camps into my game. Even just the few brief weeks I'd spent around NHL players had given me an appreciation for the finer points of the game. One of the most important takeaways that had hit home during my second camp was that scoring on an NHL goalie is a hell of a lot harder than it is in the OHL.

In junior, you can beat goalies from the top of the circle with a well-placed shot. But the best players in the world have a hard time beating even an average goalie in the NHL with the same shot. NHL goalies have sound positioning, they're big, and their equipment doesn't leave many holes. And most fans don't realize how fast NHL goalies are. In the NHL, you know that you're probably not going to beat the goalie with the first shot, and you're probably not even going to beat him on the second shot, either, because he can move so quickly to reposition himself after the rebound— Jonathan Quick in Los Angeles is the best at it; he will battle right to the end. Most of the time in the NHL, you're going to have to get a third chance to score.

Of course, all that time you're trying to score on second and third chances, the other team's defensemen are doing whatever they have to do to clear the front of the net. Guys block shots in the OHL, but not as often as they do in the NHL. Getting a shot through is probably the hardest part of trying to score goals in the NHL. There are very few players in the NHL who can walk off the half wall and beat a goalie clean. So I was excited to learn how to score goals in new ways.

Armed with that knowledge, I had a ton of confidence for my final year of junior hockey. And it paid off. A couple of weeks after I got back to London, we had a game in Kitchener. Not only did we win that night, but I had a couple of goals and two assists. I could feel things clicking on the ice in a way that I never had before.

There was a great energy to the team that year. Mitch Marner had joined the Knights the year before, and even at that young age, his skills were unreal. He was a natural leader, and there wasn't anything he couldn't do with the puck. Watching guys like Mitch and Christian Dvorak develop their game and seeing the passion they brought motivated me to work that much harder. And they were just two of the many players from the Knights who would go on to break into the NHL during that period. It was a special time, and I wanted to make the most of it.

At the same time that I was starting to learn ways to score more effectively, my understanding and control of my diabetes was also getting better. For me, when I'm low, it can take up to fifteen minutes after I eat or drink something until my blood sugar levels are back to normal. I'd known that for a while, but still, those fifteen minutes could feel like an eternity as my body processed the sugar in my system. Mentally, I could push myself through some of the lows, but I finally accepted that it was essential that my body be in the same state as my mind. As frustrating as it might be at times, I understood that I had to let my body catch up to my mind if I was going to perform at my best.

Before that year, when I went low in a hockey game, I would be in a foul mood for the full fifteen minutes as I waited for my blood sugar to come back up. It would affect how I acted on the bench and how I performed on the ice. My teammates must have hated it. But as my willpower got stronger and stronger throughout the season, I learned how to control my own actions and reactions. The moment I saw someone about to give me some Gatorade or some juice, even if I physically felt like garbage, I accepted their help, and then I could walk myself through the next few minutes, visualizing what would happen and telling myself that everything would be all right. Before I knew it, my blood sugar would bounce back up, and I would be ready to roll again. It seemed I had finally come to a point in my life where I was prepared and responsible.

Late into my final season with the Knights, our team was about to head on a road trip. Like I did before every road trip, I lay down for a nap for a few hours before the bus left. Shortly before I had to be at the rink, Gail called upstairs to me, telling me it was time to get ready. A few minutes later, she yelled up to say it was almost time to go.

"Max, did you hear me?" Gail asked.

When I didn't answer, Gail asked Scott to go upstairs and check on me. A few seconds later, he called down.

"Gail, you need to come up here," Scott yelled.

Gail went running upstairs and joined Scott. They could see right away what had happened: I had gone low. I was sweating like crazy—it looked like someone had thrown a bucket of water on me—and I was almost completely unresponsive. They tried to get me to drink some juice, but I refused and held my teeth together. Scott grabbed their emergency glucagon—an ugly needle long enough to pierce through clothing—which they kept on hand for exactly this sort of situation.

Gail started mixing the dose, while Scott tried to hold me still so that he could deliver the needle.

"Stop it!" I yelled as I rolled around. I kept trying to pull the blankets up to cover myself. I wasn't acting rationally, and I didn't know what I was doing, so I couldn't recognize that Scott and Gail were trying to save me. I was so out of it that I wouldn't even remember what happened until Gail and Scott told me about it after.

They finally rolled me onto my stomach so that they could inject the glucagon into my butt cheek. I was still thrashing around, but they eventually managed to jab in the needle.

"That hurts!" I yelled at the top of my lungs.

I immediately rolled away from Scott and Gail. They desperately tried to keep me on my stomach—they were afraid the needle would bend or break off inside me if I rolled too far. Gail climbed onto the far side of the bed and tried to push me back toward Scott so that he could take out the needle. But I wouldn't stop putting up a fight.

Finally, out of desperation, Gail slapped me in the face to calm me down. It didn't work. I laughed manically, like I was the Joker from Batman, but I still wouldn't roll back over.

"Smarten up, Max," Gail said as she slapped me again. That second one quieted me down enough for Scott to finish the injection and get the needle out.

Within a few minutes of the injection, I started to come around. I looked up at Gail and Scott beside me. "What's going on?" I asked.

Gail was huffing and puffing, because even after the slap, she and Scott still had to use all their strength to hold me down and make sure the needle came out safely.

I felt awful when they told me what had happened. I didn't want to be a burden on them, and clearly it had been an ordeal. I thanked them, had a shower, and got dressed, while Gail and Scott phoned my family to fill them in on what had happened—any time anything diabetes-related happened, Gail and Scott let my parents know. My mom was usually pretty relaxed, but my dad could often get more worked up, and I knew he'd be extra worried after this recent episode.

Gail called the team and told them that I was going to be late for the bus, and when I'd recovered enough to head out, Scott drove me over. I still felt awful—it would be days before I felt back to normal—but I was determined to head out with the team on our road trip.

Steve Sullivan, who is now the Coyotes' assistant general manager, was a development coach for us at the time, and he kept tabs on me after I got sent back to London. Steve helped me deal with the stress of being cut from the Coyotes training camp and kept me focused on working on my game and becoming more NHL-ready.

More than anything else, though, what Steve helped me understand was that every type of adversity has to be handled differently. You have to deal with each challenge—whether it's being cut from a team, being diagnosed with diabetes, or your parents divorcing—one at a time. And every challenge makes you stronger and teaches you how to deal with the next one. Becoming an NHL player isn't all roses—it can suck at some points. Setbacks are going to happen. It's how you choose to meet all those different challenges that matters.

Thankfully, I was about to be given a chance to rise to one of the greatest challenges for a young hockey player—the World Juniors. I was invited to the summer tryouts for that year's team. I was confident again heading into the tryouts, given how I'd been playing the past few months. But underneath that confidence was a bundle of nerves. The memory of being cut the year before still stuck with me. What if the coaches didn't see a spot for me on the team again? What if I suddenly went low and couldn't perform during the tryouts?

Face the challenges one at a time, I reminded myself. *Show them you belong here.*

Finally, on a snowy Saturday in December 2014, the day of the announcement arrived. I was hanging in the basement of our family home in Toronto, half of my attention on social media and the other half on TSN on the TV in front of me. Suddenly my phone rang—it was an official from Hockey Canada. I'd been selected for the final World Junior camp, right before the tournament.

We spoke for less than a minute, and I barely heard anything they said after "Congratulations." Compared to the pain of having been cut the year before, this phone call felt like winning the lottery. I'd dreamed about playing for Team Canada for so long, and now that dream was that much closer to coming true.

When I'd finished calling everyone and anyone I knew to share the news, I turned back to the TV to watch a World Junior special with James Duthie and Bob McKenzie. The ticker at the bottom of the screen was listing the names of the other players who had been invited to that final camp. As I saw the roster scroll by, I grinned. *This is going to be a really good team*, I thought. All my nerves transformed into pure excitement. I just wanted the tournament to start so we could try to win the gold medal.

I felt even better when I walked into the dressing room a few weeks later, and the first person I saw was Anthony Duclair. I had first met Anthony at the Ivan Hlinka Tournament for Under-Eighteens a few years before, and we'd gotten along right away. Out on the ice at the World Junior tryouts, we worked together in a couple of drills, and all I could think was, *Wow, this guy can play!* We complemented each other's game and style of play, and when the coaches partnered us with Sam Reinhart—or Rhino, as we called him—for scrimmages, we found great chemistry. Sam is a huge centerman whose hockey IQ is through the roof. He could play on both sides of the rink and in every situation, and he created a lot of space for the rest of the line. Duclair is blazing fast and a pure goal scorer—you get him the puck in the right area and he'll score.

All three of us made it through the team's final cuts. The tournament was split between Montreal and Toronto that year, and the stakes were high. Canada hadn't won a medal in either of the past two tournaments, and more important, they hadn't won a gold in five years. There was a lot of pressure for us to bring home some hardware—our mind was set on the gold, but some people felt that anything would do.

We tried not to let that pressure get to us. Along with being a great line mate, Duclair was a lot of fun to hang out with off the ice. We talked about how we would avoid getting wound up before games, and we decided that our thing at the World Juniors that year would be going to the spa together. The first time we went was when Team Canada was training in Niagara Falls. The hotel we were staying at had a high-end spa, and Anthony and I visited it at least twice while we were there. We would get a massage, a manicure, and a pedicure. Afterward, Anthony would cruise around the hotel in a robe—he had no shame, and the guys thought it was hilarious, which kept things relaxed.

Our team that year was a powerhouse. We won our four round robin games, and we only gave up four goals the entire time. Then we crushed Denmark and Slovakia by a combined score of 13–1 in the quarter- and semifinals. We were flying high.

The energy was infectious on the ice. Early on in the tournament I scored a goal, and in the celebration afterward, for whatever reason, I stuck my tongue out and started laughing. I wasn't trying to be disrespectful or anything—I almost didn't know I was doing it the first time. But the boys on the team thought it was hilarious, and the next thing I knew, it was my trademark celebration.

The celebratory atmosphere spilled off the ice and into the stands. During games I almost never look into the crowd—I want to remain focused on what's happening in front of me and stay present with my teammates. But during one round robin game, after we scored, I could sense a person staring at me. Before high-fiving my teammates, I looked to my right into the stands. There, I made eye contact with my uncle Ori, who was standing and cheering me on. It was an incredible moment—I felt so proud and lucky that my family was right there with me.

After our wins in the quarter- and semifinals, we were set for a showdown with Russia in the gold medal game. You couldn't ask for anything more than that as a player. My mom, dad, and sisters were all at the game at the ACC.

On January 5, 2015, while the rest of the nation was gathering around their TVs or making their way to the arena for that night's championship game, I was doing what I always did before a game— pricking my finger and testing my blood to make sure my blood sugar level was exactly where it needed to be. I'd been constantly testing all day long to make sure my levels were in the proper range, and I wasn't about to slip up, not with so much at stake. I knew my emotions could easily make it a challenge to stay in the right range that day, but I had to keep myself as stable as I could. This was the biggest game of my life.

Looking back on not just the game but that entire day, I wish

I would have been able to enjoy it more and take it all in. I was so focused on the game, keeping my blood sugar level normal, and getting dialed in that I wasn't really enjoying everything happening around me. My family were texting me, sending me photos of them decked out in Team Canada gear and describing the party that fans were having outside the arena. I was pumped, and I felt my heart rate spike every time a new message came in, but I told myself to treat it like any other game day.

As I entered the rink for the pregame warm-up, I reflected on what had happened over the past year. Twelve months earlier I had been absolutely gutted after hearing the news that I'd been cut from Team Canada. Now here I was, about to step onto the ice at Air Canada Centre, my dad's old rink, playing for Team Canada in the gold medal game for the World Juniors.

Unlike anyone else on Team Canada, I knew every inch of the ACC. When I was a kid, I would sometimes jump into the hot tub in the Leafs dressing room while my dad was on the ice for practice. Fast forward to that night, and I was back in the hot tub again before our warm-up, this time as a player so I could try to calm my nerves. I looked around at the photos of previous Leafs rosters hanging on the wall, and a wave of déjà vu hit me as I realized that the room looked exactly the same as when I was a kid.

After I got out of the hot tub, I tested my blood again. My levels were a little high, all because I was super-excited for the game to start—when your adrenaline is ramped up, your blood sugar can rise with it. I wasn't too concerned, though. In a game like that, I would rather start a little higher so that I have a buffer, knowing that my blood sugar level is going to come down. When I tested my blood again just before the game started, my numbers were at the perfect level for me to start flying the moment the puck dropped.

It wasn't only me; the whole dressing room was just so pumped as we got ready to play that night. During our pregame meal, I pulled Anthony Duclair aside.

"We have to do something to get this crowd into it right away, man," I said.

"What are you thinking?" he asked.

"We need to get the Russians going. At the opening face-off, I'm going to turn and give the Russian beside me a whack. As soon as I do that, he's going to do the same to me. Then you do the same to your winger."

Anthony smiled. "I like it. Let's do it."

A few minutes before we headed out for our warm-ups, Coach Benoit Groulx came in to give us his pregame speech. He kept it simple. He looked at us and said, "You've been working towards this night for a long, long time. Don't think too much and have fun out there. You know what you need to do. So go do what you've been working for your whole life."

It was the perfect thing to say in that moment, and every one of us in that room was pushing hard for the guy next to him. Usually on teams like these, at least the ones that I've been a part of, you don't come together as a team quite as much as you would in the regular season because you only have a short time together. But Team Canada that year, we came together quickly and became really close. Each of us trusted that the next guy was going to do his job, and we knew we had the support of the entire country behind us.

When it was game time against the Russians and we walked onto the ice, the arena was absolutely packed with cheering fans. When I left the dressing room the chants were a distant rumble, but with each step toward the ice they became louder. When my skates hit the ice, the roar of the fans washed out everything else.

Holy shit, is this really happening? I thought as I skated a few laps. The whole arena was painted red and white, from the video screens to the jersey that every fan seemed to be wearing. I had always wanted to play in front of a crowd like that, in a game with international stakes, and here I was. It was like a dream come true.

Rhino, Anthony, and I had started every game in the tournament, so I knew we would be out there to start the gold medal game. Sure enough, we were tipped to start the game. As we lined up at center ice, I looked over at Anthony—it was time to poke the Russian bear.

The Russians did exactly what we wanted them to do and poked us back. As we waited for the opening face-off, I speared the Russian, and he cross-checked me in the head. Anthony did the same thing and got a similar reaction, and the referees raced over to break up all four of us. The linesman had to keep standing between me and the Russian winger to stop us from going at it. It was perfect—the ACC crowd went nuts.

The puck dropped, and we sent it deep into their zone. Anthony picked up the puck and won a battle along the half wall on the left wing, then passed it down low to me near the goal line. I sidestepped a defenseman as Sam went to the net and Anthony cut to the hash marks. I fed Anthony a pass under the Russian defenseman's stick, and with one motion he smoothly caught the puck a little behind him and ripped it far side for a beauty goal. The ACC went absolutely bananas. It was twenty-three seconds into the first period, and we had a 1–0 lead.

Anthony skated toward our bench to celebrate, and I raced over from behind the net to join him. Anthony had this massive smile, and as our line all piled around him we were so fired up, all we could do was scream. The thrill of that first shift had everyone jacked up.

After that shift, it seemed like everything seemed to be happening for us. We went up 2–0 a couple of minutes later on a beautiful tip by Nick Paul that had the fans on their feet. But the Russians scored later in the period, cutting our lead in half at the end of the first frame.

During the intermission, though, the guys in the dressing room weren't worried at all. We still felt the game was ours to win, and we were determined to make that happen.

Five minutes into the second period, Josh Morrissey sprang Connor McDavid on a breakaway with an incredible pass. There's fast, and then there's Connor McDavid fast. Connor blew by the Russians and made no mistakes. We were back up by two.

Then, just before the halfway mark of the game, I had a chance of my own. I cruised down the left wing with the puck as Sam pretended to cut to the net. Using him as a decoy, I pulled the puck toward my body and fired a wrist shot that flew into the net under the Russian goalie's arm. I pounded both fists on the boards and hugged my teammates as they crowded around me.

It seemed like nothing could stop us. Not long after I scored, Sam and I went on a rush to the Russians' end. I took a harmless shot toward the net, and Sam got a stick on it, tapping the puck just enough to mess with the goalie and squeeze through his five-hole for a goal.

At that point, we felt we were in complete control of the game and that we had it in the bag. But the Russians weren't giving up. They scored three times, bringing our lead to a narrow 5–4.

I can only imagine how nervous everyone who was watching the game from the outside felt. But inside the team, we weren't worried. Coach Benoit Groulx was a funny guy. He had a French accent and he could never say "tic-tac-toe" properly. It always came out like "tic-tac-tao." It became a running joke throughout the tournament.

Teemu Selanne holding me in my earliest days.

You're never too young to learn. From the moment I could hold a hockey stick in my hands, I dreamed of playing hockey.

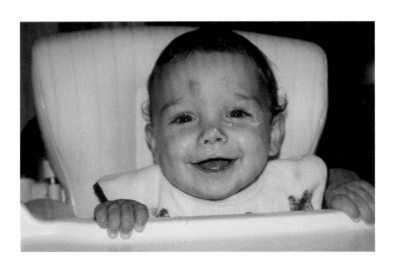

Some of my favorite childhood memories are from the moments I spent hanging out in Maple Leaf Gardens and the Air Canada Centre, learning from the amazing guys my dad played with. Mats Sundin, in particular, was one of my biggest heroes.

Me with my family in younger, more carefree days before my type 1 diabetes diagnosis. I have always been close with my mom, Leanne; my dad, Tie; my older sister, Carlin; and my younger sister, Avery.

As a kid, all I wanted to do was play hockey. If I wasn't on the ice, I was strapping on my Rollerblades and practicing my shot in the garage or on the driveway.

This was the last full season I played before I was diagnosed with type 1 diabetes (front row, second from left). It was a difficult learning process—I wanted to keep competing and be treated just like any other kid, but my diabetes meant that I always had to be thinking and preparing differently. Luckily, I had amazing teammates, coaches, and friends to help me along the way. *Upper Canada College*

Here I am celebrating with Charlie Graham. After I joined the Don Mills Flyers, I changed my jersey number to 16 as a tribute to Bobby Clarke. He had type 1 diabetes, too, but he was a legend in the NHL, and he inspired me to keep chasing my dream.

When my dad called me and said that Wayne Gretzky would be dropping by my practice in London, Ontario, I didn't know whether or not to believe him. But sure enough, the Great One was there, and getting to spend some time with him was priceless. *Claus Andersen*

I've met and learned from some amazing players, including Mario Lemieux, who has shared some of his thoughts on the game. He really inspired me by battling back from cancer to play hockey and made me believe that having type 1 diabetes wouldn't stop me from living my dreams.

It was amazing winning the Robertson Cup and celebrating with Uncle Ori and Aunt Trish, who are like second parents to me.

I was still buzzing from Bo Horvat's last-second goal in Game 7 of the 2013 OHL Finals when I lifted the Robertson Cup for the second time in two years. Playing with the London Knights in the OHL showed me what it was going to take to become a professional hockey player. More than that, it showed me that to do that, I would have to put my health before anything else. *Claus Andersen/Getty Images*

Getting drafted to the NHL had been my dream since I was three years old. In 2013, that dream came true when the Phoenix Coyotes drafted me with their first-round pick. *Bruce Bennett/Getty Images*

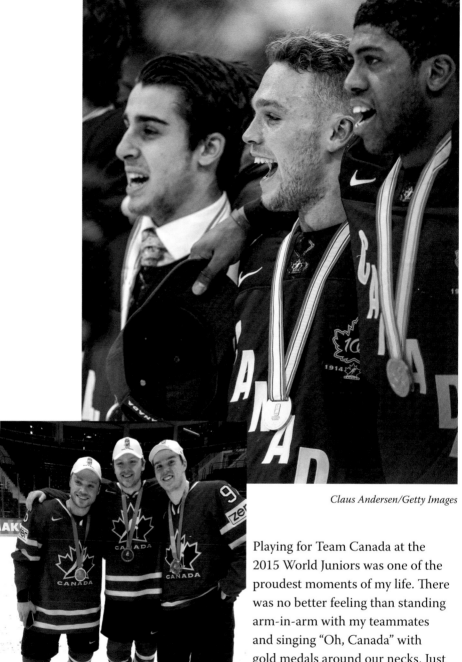

Claus Andersen/Getty Images

Playing for Team Canada at the 2015 World Juniors was one of the proudest moments of my life. There was no better feeling than standing arm-in-arm with my teammates and singing "Oh, Canada" with gold medals around our necks. Just sixteen months later, I got to do it all again in the World Men's Championship, reunited with Sam Reinhart and Connor McDavid.

Harry How/Getty Images

My first couple of years in the NHL had ups and downs. I thought I had a handle on my diabetes management when I entered the league, but I quickly learned that, if I was going to sustain my career in the NHL, I had to take my preparation to a whole new level. Thankfully, I had people like my teammate and friend Jakob Chychrun (left) to help me through that time.

Orion, my diabetes alert dog, is one of my best friends. He can detect changes to my blood sugar level through scent and can warn me if I'm going high or low, but he's also an invaluable emotional support—the moment I see him after a long day or a tough game, I forget any frustrations I might have.

I've always been lucky to learn from amazing mentors, including my manager, Allen, who's helped me through so much in my life.

Dr. Anne Peters is a world-class diabetes specialist, and she has helped me fine-tune my diabetes management in ways I never would have thought possible. Along the way, she's become like a second mom to me.

When I was traded to the Montreal Canadiens in June 2018, I knew I was joining a team with an amazing legacy. Every time I pull on that jersey, I feel a sense of pride and honor to be a part of that. *Francois Lacasse/NHLI via Getty Images*

Me with my mom and my sisters, Carlin and Avery (top), and me with my Nena; my sister, Carlin; my cousin, Devan; my uncle, Dash; and my sister, Avery (bottom, left to right). And me with my grandparents, Harold and Connie Coker. To this day, my family remains one of my biggest supports, and I'm so thankful for all of the sacrifices they've made over the years to help me get to where I am today.

I've always believed that with every challenge comes an opportunity, and meeting kids at JDRF events like this is a reminder of that. Living with type 1 diabetes has made me a stronger, better person, and it's never stopped me from following my dreams. And it doesn't have to stop anyone else from achieving their dreams, either. *Nick Lafontaine*

When the Russians were starting to make it close, Groulx called a time-out. As we gathered around the bench, he looked around at the team, all of us expecting him to give us some big speech. Instead, he just said, "Tic-tac-tao." We laughed, and the stress was immediately gone.

The same atmosphere held in the dressing room during the second intermission. We were still in the lead, and we had just twenty minutes left to play. All we had to do was play our game, and we'd win the thing.

The third period was tense. There was a ton of back-and-forth and multiple chances for both us and the Russians. But neither of us could crack the other's goalie that period. Finally, with 3.9 seconds left, there was a final face-off in our end. I was on the bench, but I knew we were in good hands because Rhino was taking the draw on his strong side.

I've seen him win this type of face-off tons of times, he is not going to lose it, I thought as I sat on top of the boards of our bench, waiting to jump onto the ice for the celebration.

Sure enough, Sam won the draw, we held the puck for the last few seconds, and as the final buzzer sounded, the arena exploded.

The whole team flew toward our goalie, Zach Fucale. I don't know who got to him first, but it was a mob scene. We were jumping up and down and screaming nonstop. At the end of it, we would barely be able to speak.

When we finally settled down, we lined up on the blue line for the awards ceremony. A gold medal was hung around each of our necks, and our captain, Curtis Lazar, hoisted the trophy above his head at center ice as the fans roared. We were smiling ear to ear as the whole arena sang the national anthem. All of us were such bad singers, but to stand arm-in-arm with your teammates and sing

"O Canada" in your own country after winning a gold medal is an emotional moment.

After the medals were handed out, they announced the tournament awards, and I was shocked to hear my name called as the tournament's top forward. As I skated out to accept the award, I heard a rumbling around me. "Domi, Domi, Domi," the crowd chanted. I felt a shiver roll down my spine. My dad used to joke that nothing compares to hearing your name chanted at the ACC. He was right!

I was on such a high when I got to the dressing room. We all were. We had a quick celebration, just the players, coaches, and staff, and then we had to go out and do media. I was talking with reporters, ushers, fans, and staff, and I got totally caught up in the conversations. Eventually, I realized I had half of my gear still on, so I headed back to the change room, where I discovered most of the guys had already gone upstairs to celebrate with their families and friends.

"Oh, no, I forgot to ask everyone for their sticks!" I said. I was a big fan of collecting the sticks of guys that I played with. I took off my skates and ran upstairs, where I went around the room, half of my gear still on, asking guys to sign their stick for me.

"What are you doing?" Rhino asked. "Go shower and get dressed!"

I finally got all my sticks and then quickly showered and changed. My whole family was waiting for me upstairs. My parents, my sisters, and my aunt and uncle all gathered me into a huge hug the moment they saw me—I was moved at just how excited they were.

It wasn't a crazy party afterward, which gave me a chance to sit back and let it all sink in. My phone was constantly buzzing with messages of congratulations. One of them stood out to me—it was from Mats Sundin.

Congrats Maxie

Happy for you, well deserved, enjoy it.

Mats

The moment I saw that text, I became a seven-year-old kid again. It meant the world to me.

Of course, my diabetes didn't care that it was the greatest night of my life, and I had to take a break from the party a couple of times to check my blood sugar. My attention to my diabetes throughout the tournament had paid off, and that discipline couldn't suddenly end when it was time to celebrate.

A few months later, the team got back together at a ceremony to receive our World Juniors rings. It was a great day—it was mixed in with a celebration for the Men's World Championship, which Canada had also won that year—and we were having a blast catching up. The problem was I was laughing and having so much fun with the boys that I wasn't paying attention to my diabetes. We went out that night after the ring ceremony, and right when I was in the middle of celebrating and having fun, my blood sugar dropped and I went low. It ended up being a rough night. It wasn't a fun experience for me, and the next morning I was in bad shape, but thankfully I had people around me to help me out. I was lucky.

As a person with type 1 diabetes, if I was going to drink alcohol, I had to be smart about it. That night was a reminder that even in the most celebratory moments I could never let things get out of hand, that my health came first and I had to respect my limits. If I wanted the privileges of being an adult, then I had to act like one.

•   •   •

When I got back to the Knights after the World Juniors, I had a new perspective. I was twenty years old, and some of my teammates were only sixteen. I realized that guys like Colin Martin had been right—your time in junior goes by so fast.

We were a young team but a good one, and we were making a push as we got ready for the playoffs. I often thought back to what Dave Tippett told me before I was sent down that season—"Become a leader." As the captain of the team, I saw it as my responsibility to help as many young players as possible.

There's always a need to earn your stripes, but hockey is a team sport, and every person on that team matters. We needed everyone if we were going to be successful. So, in my final year in London, I made sure not to treat anyone differently just because it was his first year in the league. I tried to listen to each of the younger players and show him that I cared and genuinely wanted to know how he felt about certain situations. Everyone had a role.

To help bring the team together as we entered the playoffs, Matt Rupert, a couple of other guys, and I decided to pick a haircut that the whole team would get together. We decided to get Mohawk hairdos inspired by Chuck Liddell, the UFC fighter. We thought it would be hilarious, but I ended up looking like a criminal. Still, when twenty-three of us walked into an arena, all with the same crazy Mohawk, it sent a message: we were in this together.

I found I enjoyed that last period in London so much more because of all the challenges I had embraced. Although we didn't go far in the playoffs that year—we lost to Erie in the second round—I had the best season of my OHL career. It wasn't about points, though. At the end of the season, I was honored with the Mickey Renaud Trophy, given to a team captain who best exemplifies passion and leadership. Of course, everyone wants to score goals and win championships and all that. But when you get rewarded for something that speaks to who you are, not just what you can do, that's just as good. Especially when it represents someone like Mickey.

Mickey had been the captain of the Windsor Spitfires, but he'd died in 2008 from a heart condition. When I received the trophy, I got to meet Mickey's parents. It was a touching moment, and it hit home for me—here was a family whose son had wanted to do nothing but play hockey. Mickey had dedicated his life to hockey and to helping those around him, and I saw that I had a chance to do the same.

It capped off what had been an amazing year. The gold medal at the World Juniors had given me a taste of some of the biggest honors you could win on the ice. And at the end of the OHL season, I was starting to see what sort of leader I wanted to be. I felt lucky to have been a part of those special events. But even with how far I'd come, there was still much more to go. I still hadn't realized my dream of making the NHL. I'd been given all of the tools and experience I could ask for. Now it was time to put them to work.

8

PREPARATION IS A SECRET WEAPON

By September 2015, I was ready for anything. I flew down to Arizona for my third training camp with the Coyotes, and this time things were different. The only realistic options for me were playing in the NHL or with the Coyotes' minor league affiliate in the AHL. Technically, I could have been sent back to the OHL for an overage year, but the likelihood of that happening was small. I made a promise to myself that I wouldn't end up playing in the AHL. I was going to make sure I was in the NHL to stay.

The moment I stepped on the ice for our first skate, I felt different. I never let my focus waver for a single second of any practice. There was no drill, no shift, and no scrimmage off. By then I knew that I was being evaluated every moment, on and off the ice, and I was going to make sure that the coaches saw the best of me. When you're under the microscope, you can't afford any slipups.

I found it inspiring that the hardest-working guys in camp were the ones who were already guaranteed a spot on the team. I tried to model my behavior after those veterans, people like Oliver Ekman-Larsson and Shane Doan—they showed me that it would take commitment not just to make it to the NHL, but to stay there.

In the NHL, it's not just the forty-five-minute practice or sixty-minute game that matters. It is all about what you do twenty-four hours prior to that game or twenty-four hours after; your preparation beforehand and your recovery process afterward. And the timing becomes that much more important when you throw type 1 diabetes into the mix.

The older guys would often tell me, "You're going to have a blast, but it is not like junior." It reminded me of Colin Martin telling me that junior would go by fast. I wondered how this would be different.

In a lot of ways, I was still in junior hockey mode. In junior, after practice, if the team hung out, it was typically the whole team that hung out. We would all go out and see a movie, eat sushi—whatever we did, we all did it together. Most guys in junior are in their late teens, so other than the fact that some of the younger players have school, we didn't have many distractions other than hockey or each other.

I quickly saw that it wasn't that way in the NHL. Sure, the rookies or younger players on the team would hang out together. But the majority of the guys had a wife and kids at home, so after they were done at the rink, they'd go home to be with their family. Hockey was their job, and they treated it seriously. It was a totally different environment.

My house turned into a hangout spot for a lot of the younger players. They'd come over to have food or just to chill after practice. I loved it—it gave us a chance to get to know each other, and it helped me with the transition out of junior.

Of course, at some point I had to have my welcome-to-the-NHL wake-up moment. Every player does, no matter how good they are.

Mine came during a preseason game against the L.A. Kings. I lost Drew Doughty in our defensive zone and he wheeled behind me, dished a perfect backhand pass to his teammate, and the Kings scored an easy goal. It was clearly my fault, and my first thought was, *Shit, so that's what it feels like to get burned in the NHL.*

I wanted to get my revenge, but we wouldn't be playing the Kings until a few weeks later, when we'd face them for our first regular season game. But I didn't know if I'd still be with the team at that point. I didn't want my reputation to be one of defensive lapses, so I dialed up my intensity the next few games.

After our last preseason game, the coaching staff made their final cuts. When I discovered the announcements had gone out and that I hadn't been sent home, it took a minute for my brain to process what that meant: I was going to be on the opening night roster.

I immediately called my mom and dad.

"Guys, I made it!" I said. "I'm going to be on the opening night roster."

"That's amazing!" my mom said. "Congratulations! I'm so happy for you."

"Now the real work starts," my dad said. I could tell my dad was happy for me, too, but I wasn't surprised that he was already focused on the game ahead against a roster full of Stanley Cup champions.

My whole family flew down to the game in L.A. My mom, my dad, my sisters, my cousin Jeff, my uncle Dash, and a couple of my closest buddies, Robert Adamo and Angelo Nitsopoulos, whom I'd known since I was a kid, were all at the Staples Center in Los Angeles that night when I made my official NHL debut.

Before the game started, I was caught up in a flurry of nerves and excitement. I was about to play in my first NHL game, something I had dreamed of my entire life. I tried to stay calm. I wanted to be ready in every way, not the least of which included my blood sugar levels.

When the puck dropped, I tried to settle into a rhythm and keep my head clear—I didn't want to make another mistake like the one I made in the preseason against Doughty. A few minutes into the second period, I had jumped over the boards and taken a couple of hard strides into L.A.'s zone when the puck got knocked loose and ended up on my stick. The rest of the play was pure instinct. I took two quick steps toward the center of the ice and unleashed a wrist shot that beat Jonathan Quick top corner for my first NHL goal. I saw the puck drop behind Quick and I threw both of my hands up in the air. I didn't know what to do with myself. The first person I saw was Antoine Vermette, so I just jumped into his arms as the rest of our line swarmed us.

"Easy game, eh, bud?" Steve Downie said jokingly as we got back to the bench. Truth be told, I was barely processing what was happening to me. The whole thing had happened so fast, it was a blur. Still, it was a dream come true. The guys on the bench were genuinely fired up for me—you only score your first NHL goal once. Even better, we won the game 4–1 to start the season on a high note.

A few weeks later was an even bigger night for me and my family. It was October 26, 2015, and it was my first game at the Air Canada Centre as an NHL player. I wanted to beat the Leafs so badly. I felt like I had a rivalry with the team because of my dad's history with them.

Given that, it felt like an odd sort of homecoming. I told myself all day not to get too caught up in the past and to treat the game like any other, because despite the hype it was just another game we had to win.

With the way my nerves were flying up and down that day, I ended up testing my blood a few extra times to make sure my levels were good. When I tested my blood just before the game, I was around a 3, which was low for me. Despite all of my efforts to stay on top of my diabetes, my emotions that day had still caused my blood sugar level to drop. Just like every other day, I had to confront my diabetes before I could succeed on the ice.

I drank some juice to bring my blood sugar up, and a few minutes later I was ready to go. Now it was up to me to just go out and play the game in the building that had been my second home for years.

At the start of the game, our goalie Mike Smith got me good.

"Max, you go out there first," he said.

"Thanks, Smitty," I said. I should have seen what was about to happen—it was a classic hockey joke to make the rookie on the team skate a lap by himself when he first played in his hometown. But I was so excited—this felt like my first NHL game all over again—that I didn't clue in.

I headed down the hallway, proud and happy, and I leapt onto the ice and started flying. As I came around the net, though, I realized I was alone on the ice. The rest of the guys were laughing like crazy in the hallway as I skated around by myself. I must have had a good eight laps before the rest of the team joined me, and I was so embarrassed that I don't think I once hit the net with a shot the entire time. But when I got back into the dressing room, I collected myself, and by the time I went out for the anthems, I was locked in again.

Throughout the next sixty minutes, I could have sworn I was having flashbacks to all the games I had watched from the stands while my dad was playing for the Leafs. In fact, the whole game was a giant flashback. At one point I glanced up at the video scoreboard that hangs above center ice at the ACC. If you look up there, you will see a big maple leaf under the screen. When my dad brought me to the ACC as a kid, I would often go out on the ice by myself with a bucket of pucks right before the morning skate. I'd dump the pucks on the fresh ice and look at the empty seats around me, thinking, *One day, I'm going to play here and all of these seats will be full.* Being back in the exact same place, looking up at the same maple leaf, it felt surreal that day had finally come.

Not long into the first period, we went on the power play. I lined up along the boards in the Leafs' end next to Morgan Reilly, whom I'd played with at a summer World Junior camp a few years prior.

"What's up, bud?" he said as we waited for the puck to drop. "Slow down."

I laughed—I heard it a lot in the NHL, guys telling me to slow down as a joke.

"Good to see you, too, man," I said.

After the draw, the puck was knocked toward us along the half wall. I beat Reilly to the puck and dropped it back to the point. We set up our umbrella and started to move the puck around. Michael Stone fed the puck back to me. I took a few steps toward the net with the puck rolling on my stick and then, just as I reached the face-off dot, I fired it at the net as hard as I could. I didn't have time to aim, but the puck flew to the opposite top corner to give us a 1–0 lead.

I was so fired up, to score a goal at the same rink my dad had called home for all those years. I couldn't see my family up in their box that night, but I was happy to imagine them cheering and high-fiving. I knew they were as excited as I was.

Early in my rookie season, the older players noticed that everyone else on the team would already be dressed and ready to go by the time I got to the room to put my gear on. I was the same as my dad—I didn't want to be sitting around with my thoughts before the game. That would only make me nervous, which could throw off my blood sugar. Any extra time I had at the rink before the game I spent managing my diabetes, so putting on my equipment was the easy part of getting ready.

It all comes down to preparation. When I first get to the rink, I set up my equipment the exact same way. When it's time to hit the ice, I start by throwing on my long johns and grab a T-shirt. My pants are in front of me, shin pads and socks on one side and my jock on the other. I put new laces in my skates every game, and I tie my skates tight—I loosen them enough to slide them on and then only have to tighten up the top three eyelets to be ready.

From start to finish it takes four and a half minutes, and then I'm grabbing my stick by the dressing room door and walking out to the ice with my teammates.

I break down every NHL game into parts. I treat every period like it's a mini-game. And within that period, there's a TV time-out every five minutes, so I divide the period into quarters. Each break gives me an opportunity to check in with myself, see how my blood sugar level feels, and make any adjustments needed to perform in the next part of the game.

Between periods is also all about routine. I take the top half of my gear off and walk back to the players' lounge so that I can test my blood, give myself some insulin, or have a little snack to adjust my levels. It's not that I'm embarrassed to test my blood in front of my teammates, but I like to ensure that it's not a distraction to anyone else. When I'm done, I take a few deep breaths, and as I walk back to the dressing room, I check in with the guys in the lounge who aren't playing that night.

Once I walk out of that room and shut the door, though, the switch goes back on and I am back to game mode, taping my stick and waiting for the coaches to come in for a quick meeting. When the coaches are done talking, I put on the rest of my equipment, wet my face and hair, and then I'm ready to get back to the game.

The training staff is invaluable, too—they mean everything to me. When I first started in the league, I thought I was high-maintenance because so many people were involved in making sure I was healthy and ready to go. But I quickly discovered that everyone was genuinely eager to help, which I was incredibly grateful for. If it meant helping the team win, everyone was on board. Making sure we're stocked with everything we need to treat a low and any supplies I might need, they go to incredible lengths to make sure that any potential distractions are out of the way, allowing me to focus on playing the best I can.

If we play at seven o'clock in the evening, I get to the rink around four forty-five p.m. As soon as I get there, I check my blood sugar. I test it again after our team meeting, and then again before the pregame warm-up.

Around the ten-minute mark of the first period, I test my blood on the bench. The training staff have it down to a science. They have the test strip ready in the glucose meter for me and tap me on the shoulder. I take off my glove, prick my finger, reach up, and the trainers collect the blood on the test strip for me. In five seconds they have the results, show me the number, and then I return my focus to the game. The whole thing takes ten seconds, start to finish.

If I ever need something on the bench to get my blood sugar up, every NHL team has Gatorade products on hand, from the sports drink to energy gels to chews. The training staff supplements that with other products that they find can also be helpful in delivering the carbs I need and keeping up my blood sugar levels. The trainers have everything stored neatly on the bench so that I can grab a snack or a drink anytime.

The process doesn't stop after the game ends, either. Before I speak with the media, I check my blood to make sure I'm not at risk of going too low or too high and getting irritable in an interview. Then I check my levels during the postgame workout, at the postgame meal, right after I get home, and one final time before I go to bed.

It only gets more challenging when we're on the road. When I get to a hotel, I have to make sure I have a little food and some juice on the bedside table. Again, the team trainers and staff are the best—they always make sure there's food waiting for me in my room in case I have to get my blood sugar numbers up. And the trainers always stay on the same floor as me, just in case something goes wrong in the night and they need to arrive quickly. If my insulin pump ever broke or I lost something that I needed, I could text the trainers and right away and they would be on it.

More than anything, though, I appreciated how honest the trainers and I could be with each other. Halfway through the season, one of the trainers, Jason Serbus, pulled me into his office.

"I want to tell you something," Jason said me, a serious look in his eye. "Earlier this season, I was asked by management if we had anything to worry about in regards to your diabetes and playing in the NHL. I told them that we can't have guys puking into their gloves in the middle of a game. Honestly, Max, I wasn't sure if you could keep track of your diabetes enough to play in the NHL. I didn't think you would make it."

Then Jason added something that I'll always remember. "Honestly, buddy, you've proved me wrong. I am so happy that we figured this all out. You're going to be in this league for a long time, and I'm so proud of you."

I was blown away. "Serbs," I said, "you've been a big part of why I was able to make it this far. I probably wouldn't be sitting here without you."

Jason was outstanding when it came to helping me handle my diabetes. He talked with Doug, the trainer on the Knights, to learn exactly what I needed and how to manage it. And Jason sacrificed his free time to further educate himself on type 1 diabetes, something that he wouldn't have had to do if I wasn't there. At first, we butted heads a little bit, but I quickly came to appreciate how much he cared. It was like having a parent watching over me, and I knew he wanted me to get to the next level and be an NHL hockey player. And he knew what he was talking about—he'd won a Cup with the Tampa Bay Lightning in 2004.

And it wasn't just Jason. There was also Mike Ermatinger and Mikey Griebel. All those trainers were a big part of helping me to get to where I am today. I'm thankful every minute of every day for what they did to help me get through the season. Those trainers stuck with me all the way—there's no way I could have done it alone. All of that routine and preparation helped me endure the grind that comes with playing so much, and it set me up for success.

One of the best examples of that was in January 2016. The Oilers were in town to play us at home, and we beat them 4–3 in overtime, which was the best part of the night. The second best was that I scored my first NHL hat trick.

The stats sheet tells the story of the goals—all three on the power play. The first was a tap-in that Oliver Ekman-Larsson and Stone set up. For the second, I stickhandled around a defenseman and then was able to work the puck down low. I dished the puck to Ekman-Larsson and managed to knock home his rebound. My third came off a wrist shot, and the next thing I knew, the hats were flying.

Being a young player in the NHL is a lot different than it was back in the day. One of the biggest differences is that rookies can have a bigger role on the team than they used to. Don't get me wrong, you're still a rookie and have to pay your dues. One of those was buying the veterans a nice dinner!

We had our rookie dinner at a high-end restaurant in Vancouver. I started the meal the same way I did any other—by testing my blood. When I was first diagnosed, I used to feel embarrassed when I had to take the tester out and check my blood in public. By the time of our rookie dinner, though, I had no problem—I could have pulled out a needle and stuck it in my stomach in the middle of a restaurant without blinking.

Whenever I checked my blood, I always pricked the end of one of my fingers. I had to rotate them so that I wasn't using the same one over and over. I did the same thing when it came to pump sites for my insulin. I'd use both butt cheeks and both sides of my stomach. If you inject yourself in the same place every day you can develop scar tissue, and then your body will have a problem absorbing the insulin properly. So you have to rotate the injections around your body.

The guys on the team were fine with whatever I needed to do— they were quickly getting used to it. The best part of that night was the bond that developed among our year's group of rookies. Along with me, there was Anthony Duclair and Jordan Martinook. It was a blast, and it wasn't scary at all. It ended up being a great dinner, and then we went out afterward and had a good time. Each rookie received a wine bottle signed by the whole team as a memento. I still have the bottle.

Martin Hanzal ordered the most food that night. My first impression of Hanzal was that he was a very intimidating, scary, big, grumpy guy. Once you get to know Hanzal, though, you realize that he is a great guy and that he's absolutely hilarious. He's the kind of guy who can make you laugh without even trying.

Usually during mealtime I have to count my carbs to make sure I give myself the right amount of insulin. But during our Coyotes rookie dinner I was less concerned with the food and more worried about the booze. I was just waiting for someone to pass me a shot and encourage me to drink it. I made sure I was testing my blood more frequently than usual during that night in case anything came up.

Luckily, Shane Doan was keeping an eye on me. After he noticed that I was checking my blood over and over, he quietly said to me, "Don't worry, you don't have to drink anything that is put in front of you. And if anyone has a problem with that, you come right to me." I immediately relaxed and knew that I was going to be fine.

That kind of team-bonding wasn't just fun—it was necessary. My biggest adjustment to the NHL wasn't to the strength and speed of the players. It was much more on the mental side of things.

When I lined up next to Sidney Crosby during my first home game in the NHL, I could hardly believe my luck. I had spent countless hours watching YouTube videos of the guy, and now I was playing against him. Moments like that stayed with me for days—far longer than memories of the first time being hit by a big defenseman, for example.

There were definitely some learning experiences that first year. In December 2015, we were playing in Minnesota to face the Wild. I picked up the puck in the neutral zone and was absolutely flying down the wing when I toe picked and went down. I wish I could blame the soft ice, but this one was on me. I fell and landed face-first on a defender's stick. My nose and my eye took the brunt of the fall. I came back to the bench, and I knew it wasn't good—I thought I had broken my nose, but my eyes were more messed up. I managed to get fixed up and told the coaches that I wanted to stay in the game. *There's no way I'll get hit like that again this game*, I thought, confident in my odds.

The next period, I was standing in front of the net, which was a rare occurrence for me. Connor Murphy ripped a shot along the ice, and all of a sudden Jordan Martinook stuck his stick out to tip the puck. He did tip it—straight up into my face. My whole face went numb, I couldn't feel my nose, and my eye swelled shut.

I went down right away after the puck hit me. When I was a kid, my dad would often say, "If you're hurt, get back up. If you're injured and you can't physically get up, that's a different story."

I pushed myself to my feet and skated to the bench. Once I sat down, though, I realized I was in rough shape. I wiped my face with a towel, and when I took it away, it was covered in blood. Anthony Duclair was sitting beside me, and as I looked up, I caught the shocked expression on his face, and we both started laughing. I eventually went to the dressing room to get fixed up. I looked in the mirror and saw an absolute mess—this time, my nose was actually broken. But I got everything straightened out and cleaned up, and I made it back out to the bench to finish the game. When I returned, my teammates took one look at my face and turned away. "You're a mess," one of them said with a laugh.

My dad's voice was often in my head that first year. Even though my dad and I butted heads a lot, I still called him all the time and asked him questions—I valued his opinion. And, whether I liked it or not, my dad would still send me a note before every single game. He still does it to this day. Some days he texts me a reminder to check my blood sugar levels. Other times he tells me to keep my shifts short, or to make sure I compete hard every shift (his go-to line), or to go to the blue paint, because, "Max, that's where the goals are scored."

It's more or less the same note every game, so I usually skim through it and take some mental notes here and there. But every now and then, even if it takes ten or twelve texts, I realize that what he is saying is right. Those moments are a humbling reminder that I'm lucky to have a dad who played so many years in the NHL and that I should always listen to the people around me.

Although I sometimes shrugged off my dad's texts, I knew that if I ever needed him, all I had to do was call. He was often the first person I'd reach out to when I needed reassurance. I have to say, my dad sees the game like no one else I have ever talked to. I would make a simple play during a game—something as easy as chipping the puck into the other team's zone, or skating hard toward the play off the bench—and he would notice it.

Ever since I was a kid, my dad had instilled in me the lesson that it was never acceptable to take a shift off. I might have been able to fool some people when I didn't play that well, but I could never fool my dad. Like me, he always knew when I didn't have a good game, and he wasn't afraid to let me know it. He was still holding me to the same standard he had since I was a kid—I could trust my dad to always tell me things the way they were, good or bad.

Those little details are what separate NHL players from everyone else, and you have to be aware of them at all times. For example, until you're on the ice, you can't appreciate how much chirping goes on back and forth between players. I chirp as much as the next guy. But there's an unwritten code in the NHL you have to respect—as a young player, you're not supposed to heckle older players. You have to learn when it's acceptable to chirp and when to be silent and show respect.

One night, we were playing the Senators, and as we warmed up, I remembered seeing on Twitter that it was a big milestone game for Chris Neil. As we were waiting for the first face-off, I leaned over to Neil.

"Congratulations, Chris," I said.

"Thanks a lot, buddy," he said. "How's your dad doing?"

"Oh, he's good."

"Good stuff. Say hi to him for me."

Moments like that were a reminder that, although I was excited to be in the Show, there was a history that came before me and I had to earn my place in it. Most of the time, though, I was happy to be known as a young keener. I was so excited the first time the Chicago Blackhawks came into town. Along with Crosby, Patrick Kane was my favorite player growing up. I asked my equipment manager if he would go to his counterpart on the Blackhawks and see if he could get Kane to sign a stick for me—I was too scared to ask him myself, and I figured it was a long shot. I was going to be playing against him the next day, but in that moment I was just an excited fan. I couldn't believe it when my equipment manager brought back a stick with the words "To Max. All the best, Patrick Kane" on it.

By far my favorite encounter with an older player took place one night in St. Louis when we were playing the Blues. Alex Steen of the Blues had played with my dad in Toronto. That was toward the end of my dad's career, when I was a little older and was getting to know the guys my dad played with. Steener had always been such a great guy to me—he always talked to me like I was an adult, not just one of his teammates' kids, and I'd always appreciated that.

Steen was lined up to take the face-off, and I was on the wing.

The first time we were on the ice at the same time, my centerman got kicked out of the circle and I had to step in to take the draw against Steen. As I skated in, Steen looked up and said, "What's up, Maxy? I'll see you after the game."

"Sure thing," I replied as I squatted down for the face-off.

"What's wrong with your skate?" Steen said, pointing to my laces. I was about to look down when I realized the linesman was about to drop the puck. Steen had been trying to fool me with the old "skate laces" gag. Luckily, I recovered in time to win the draw, but Steen was laughing the whole time.

My life was full of new experiences off the ice, too. Toward the end of the season, Rich Nairn, our media director, called me with a request.

"Max, there's a race car driver who's asked to meet you. He has diabetes, too, and he's in town for a race at the IndyCar racetrack outside of Phoenix. Do you have some time to go out there?"

I wasn't a big racing fan, but it sounded like fun.

"Sure, why not?" I said.

Connor Murphy, one of the other young guys on the team, went with me, and later that day we were dressed in official race suits at the side of the track, watching the Indy cars whip by during their time trials. Finally, a guy wearing a neon-green-trimmed race suit came over.

"Max, I'm Charlie Kimball," the guy said, shaking my hand.

"Nice to meet you," I said. "These cars can fly."

"Wait until you get out there and feel it for yourself," he said.

We spent the next while talking about what it was like to compete at the highest levels of our sports while managing our diabetes. There's nothing quite like the bond you have with another person who has type 1 diabetes. I mentioned how good the Coyotes trainers and doctors were, and Charlie suggested I reach out to his doctor, Dr. Anne Peters, if I had any other questions.

"She's a world-class diabetes specialist," he said. A few minutes later, someone from Charlie's team hurried up, as he was needed elsewhere. "Sorry, Max, I want to keep talking, but I need to get ready. Great to meet you. If you ever need anything, don't hesitate to reach out to me." With that, he hustled off to his car.

A track official then appeared beside me. "Head over there and grab a helmet," he said, pointing to a table at the side of the track. "The car will be here in a second"

The car pulled up, and I hopped inside.

"Just hang on to these bars," a crew member said, pointing to a couple of handles beside me. "And make sure you tuck your head a bit." He patted the driver on the shoulder and grinned. "Don't worry, you're in good hands."

We sped out onto the track and started ripping around at speeds I'd never felt before. I was relieved to see the first bend approaching, figuring we'd slow down and I could catch my breath. But Indy car drivers speed up when they go around a corner, and as we whipped around it at full speed, I was terrified that the car was going to roll right over. It was too loud for the driver to hear anything I said, so I just held on to the grips beside me for dear life.

When we finally pulled back into the pit, the driver jumped out of the car. I was shocked when I saw his gray hair and wrinkles. *That's the guy who was driving me?* I thought. Shortly after, I learned that the guy was a legend: Mario Andretti, one of the most successful racing drivers of all time. When I figured that out, I was quick to hurry over and ask for a picture.

Days like that were a nice break from the usual routine, and they gave me something fun to talk to my family about.

My mom was able to visit Arizona regularly, but I would usually catch up with my dad and sisters throughout the season at road games that they came to watch. Once, when we played the New York Islanders in Brooklyn, I found out after the game that Justin Bieber had joined my family in a box that night. Justin was a big hockey fan and had met my dad previously, so when my dad and Avery happened to run into him that day in the city, my dad invited him to the game. To my mom and sister's surprise, he actually showed up!

I checked my phone after the game and saw the photos that Avery had sent me of her and the rest of my family with Bieber. At first I thought they were fake, until they filled me in on the whole story. The visit, like most of the ones I got with my family on the road, didn't last long. We usually only had about ten minutes together after the game before I had to leave for the plane. Still, those few minutes meant the world to me. They made the grind of life on the road seem not so bad.

We didn't make the playoffs that year, so my season came to an end in April. The one silver lining was that, because I wasn't in the NHL playoffs, I was eligible to play for Team Canada at the World Hockey Championships in Russia.

I had just finished my rookie season in the NHL, so I knew I would be playing behind a lot of veterans. But still, I was excited to represent Canada again. As I packed for the trip, walking through my usual checklist once again, I thought back to the tournament I'd played in Slovakia as a teenager. I knew that I wouldn't be able to run to a local pharmacy and find exactly what I needed if something happened with my diabetes. I knew to think ahead, so I worked with the Hockey Canada staff to make sure we had every contingency planned for.

I was thrilled to be playing for Team Canada again, but I had a different role than I was used to. Sam Reinhart and I were wearing the maple leaf together again, but we were the extra forwards on the team that year. Before our first game, our coach, Bill Peters, came up to Rhino and me.

"You two know you're the extra forwards," he said. "How do you want to do it? Do you two want to rotate games? I feel bad about the whole situation."

Sam and I looked at each other. "Can we think about it?" I asked.

"Of course," Peters said.

I told Sam that I didn't mind being an extra forward, but I didn't want to be a healthy scratch.

"I get it—Corey Perry is playing ahead of me," I said. "I don't mind getting very little ice time."

"Me neither," Sam said. "But I'd rather have a little than none at all."

"Agreed."

So we went back to Peters and said we were good with being extra forwards and that we both wanted to dress for the games, even if it meant sharing a role and only playing two or three shifts a game.

It was the first time I had experienced being the extra guy on the bench, and it was a great learning experience. My attitude was that I should just focus on having fun and making sure I was ready whenever the coach tapped me on the shoulder.

When I did get on the ice, I had to make it count. In one game, I had three golden opportunities and I didn't shoot the puck. I was known as a pass-first player. In practice, I almost never shoot the puck. The boys would chirp me, "This kid won't shoot the puck. You can't score if you don't shoot the puck, Domi." Eventually, even Coach Bill Peters joined in on the fun. I'd laugh along with them— I didn't mind, and I knew my role.

In our game against Sweden, though, Sam and I found ourselves on a two-on-one. Rhino slid me a pass that I was able to bury for my one and only goal of the tournament.

The boys on the bench were so excited when I scored. When I got back to the bench, one of them yelled at me, "About time you shot the puck, Domi!"

We beat Finland in the finals to win the gold medal that year. As we were skating around the ice with the trophy, I noticed a guy with a hat on standing near the edge of the ice. I thought, *That guy looks a lot like Vladimir Putin.*

"Hey, that's Putin!" Brad Marchand yelled, at the same time that Brendan Gallagher said, "Check out Putin."

I turned to the two of them. "Let's go say hi," I said.

"No way," they said, shaking their heads.

"Fine, I'm going to say hello."

I wheeled out of the pack of players, and sure enough, Marchand and Gallagher followed behind me. We each shook his hand, and Putin just stared at us and nodded slightly. Needless to say, it wasn't quite as good a story among my friends and family—I think they preferred meeting Justin Bieber.

I might not have had my first pick of a role on the team, but winning the whole thing made it all worth it. And one thing was for certain—after that tournament, I developed a whole new sense of respect for players who only get a few minutes of ice time every game. It's a hard role to fill, but I saw that it was a more important one than I'd ever realized. The right guys there could be game-changers, the difference between a championship and an early exit.

As a kid, I used to tease my dad because he was a fourth-line player. But you forget how hard it is for a hockey player to sit that long, his body getting cold, before he has to jump on the ice. And it isn't just tough physically—it's hard mentally, too. When you're not on the ice very much, it's tough to stay engaged in the game. Being able to make an impact every time you set foot on the ice, no matter what happens before or after—now, that's a skill.

As I flew back home after the tournament, it hit me just how far I had come in a short period of time. It was only a couple of years before that I had been throwing up on the ice in the middle of a shift because I didn't have control of my diabetes. Now I was coming out of a year when I'd played eighty-one games in the NHL and been part of Team Canada at the World Hockey Championships, in Russia of all places, far away from my usual routine and the comforts of home.

I was twenty-one years old, and I had a full year in the NHL under my belt. I had also been living with type 1 diabetes for almost a decade. Nine years earlier, I had asked Dr. Strachan if I could still play hockey if I had type 1 diabetes. Not only was I still playing hockey, I was playing in the NHL. I'd finally made it.

9

ASK FOR HELP

When you're in the NHL, calling the summer the off-season is a bit misleading. There's no such thing as an "off" season. Each game in the season had made me a better player—I was getting smarter on the ice, stronger on the puck, faster on my feet. The high that came with it being my first year in the NHL had worn off, and I began to see how much work was ahead of me in all facets of my life. That summer, I decided to hit the reset button when it came to managing my body.

The first part of the summer of 2016 was all about rest and recovery as I addressed any injuries, imbalances, or weaknesses. Once I had those taken care of, it was time to get stronger and faster, so I put a plan in place with my trainer, Andy O'Brien, to get me ready for the upcoming season. Andy was one of the best in the business—he was the strength coach for the Pittsburgh Penguins, and he'd just helped the team win a Stanley Cup the year before. He also understood the impact my diabetes had on my body, so he would tailor the structure of my workouts accordingly. For Andy, it wasn't about working hard as much as it was about working smart.

I tried to bring that attitude to the rest of my conditioning that summer. One of the things I added to my workouts was Pilates. My trainer, Lisa, helped me work my body in ways I had never pushed it before. I was incredibly eager to know why I was doing each exercise and what the purpose of it was, so I was constantly pestering Lisa with questions.

I carried the same curiosity over to my diabetes management.

After I had met Charlie Kimball a few months prior, I took his suggestion seriously and reached out to Dr. Anne Peters, the Los Angeles–based diabetes specialist he recommended.

"Charlie filled me in a bit on how you helped him to develop a strategy and an understanding of how to approach his diabetes as a professional athlete," I said to Anne. "Can you help me come up with something similar for my hockey?"

Anne laughed. "I can tell you, it won't be similar," she said. "But I can definitely help."

Anne explained to me how, even though Charlie and I were both professional athletes with type 1 diabetes, our challenges and needs were completely different—what worked for Charlie would never work for me.

"We'll come up with a plan that we know works for you," she said.

After talking with Anne, I knew she was a perfect fit for me. She was committed to helping me get back on track when it came to managing my diabetes.

When my second season with the Coyotes started, I felt more confident than ever. I was strong, healthy, and ready to put my new skills to use. We started off on the right foot, winning our first game in overtime. But we lost our second game. And the one after that. And then the one following that. We were having trouble getting our season on track.

Worse, I felt like I wasn't doing my share. I wasn't able to score or set up plays. I started thinking about what I was doing on the ice rather than just doing it. Every game that went by without improvement had me more and more panicked. I was supposed to be calm, cool, and confident that I could make a play in any situation. But I was turning over the puck, bobbling passes, or just chipping the puck down the ice. I was beginning to lose every bit of confidence I had so carefully built.

Instead of taking responsibility for my play, though, I looked for easy ways out. I tried to change everything at once—I changed the curve of my stick, I bought a new house, and I started soliciting from anyone and everyone. And when that didn't work, I blamed the tools I was using or the advice I was getting. Nothing seemed to fix the problem, and it was driving me up the wall. No matter how much I complained or pointed the finger elsewhere, I couldn't bring myself to see that the real problem was in my head.

"I don't know what to do to fix this," I said to my dad during one of our regular phone calls.

"Keep working hard," he said. "Be a good teammate, and you'll get out of this funk, I promise you."

My family and teammates' support gave me the most important thing I needed during that time: confidence. If you have confidence in the NHL, you can do absolutely anything that you want. More than that, if you have confidence in life, you can do anything that you want. But as soon as you question yourself and doubt creeps in, it's over. Rebuilding confidence takes time, and it's a difficult process. But a necessary one.

So I took a step back and tried to slow things down. I focused on taking things day by day. When I wasn't at the rink, I would go for hikes, relax in my backyard, and hang out with my teammate Jakob

Chychrun, who was living with me at the time. I had volunteered to take in Jakob and help him work through the grind of being a rookie in the NHL. But when it came to making it through that period, Jakob helped me as much as I was able to help him.

And on top of those helps, I had the number one best stress relief of all time: my service dog, Orion. Orion came into my life as a DAD, or a Diabetic Alert Dog.

My mom was the first person who discovered that there are service dogs for people with diabetes. I was still a teenager at the time, and she was doing some research online on new information about diabetes when she called out, "Look, they have dogs for people with diabetes!"

I looked over her shoulder at the website, and the moment I saw the photos of all the dogs, I knew I wanted one.

"That would be amazing!" I said.

"A service dog could be very helpful in managing your diabetes," my mom said as she scrolled through the website. "Someday when you are living alone, the dog could help keep you safe."

The organization was called Canine Hope for Diabetics, and they were based in California. I read the stories about several people with type 1 diabetes and their service dogs. When a person with diabetes' blood sugar level is out of normal range, their saliva gives off a different scent. These service dogs were trained to detect that scent from the saliva. If the dog smelled that the person's blood sugar was off, they were trained to alert the person, who then knew to test their blood. Sometimes lows can happen quickly, or they happen while you're sleeping, so having a trained service dog would be another helpful management tool.

"How do you get one?" I asked as soon I'd finished reading the stories.

"It's a long application process," my mom said, looking through the requirements.

We immediately started putting together everything I'd need to apply. I had to provide detailed personal information, as well as write a series of essays just to even be considered for one of their dogs. The first essay I submitted was about why I felt I needed a service dog. The second one was about the relationship I would have with the dog—what was I expecting out of it and what could I provide for the dog. And in the third essay, I had to explain what I did for a living, how having a service dog would impact my life, and how I would take care of it.

I wasn't overly eager about writing essays—it felt like applying for a job—but I knew this was something special. I submitted the paperwork, but after some follow-up discussions with the organization, I found out that the trainer in California wasn't able to accept my application. The trainer needed to be able to remain involved in the service dog's training after placing them with a person, and Canada was just too far away for her to do that.

After I was drafted to Arizona, I figured it was time to revisit my application, since I was going to be so much closer to California. My mom reached out to Canine Hope for Diabetics again, and I was excited to hear that Crystal Keller, the founder of the organization, remembered my original application. My challenges of being an athlete living with type 1 diabetes, as well as my passion for dogs, had stuck with her. She was happy to hear I would be moving to Arizona in the future and she suggested that we fly to California to meet with her and her partner, Joanna, in person and discuss whether a DAD would be a good fit.

I still can't believe this happened, but when I met with Crystal and Joanna, my blood sugar levels went low. We were at a restaurant, and they had brought two dogs with them—one was in training, and the other belonged to Joanna, who also had diabetes. After we ordered our food, we were in that awkward stage where you are waiting for your meal to arrive and you're just trying to make small talk.

As we chatted, the dogs were lying quietly under the table, as they'd been commanded. I was confused, then, when Joanna's dog got up and put her head on my lap. I didn't know what to do, so I looked at Joanna.

"Is it normal for the dog to be putting her head on me like this?" I asked.

"She's acting strangely—something must be up. Maybe I'm low," Joanna said. She tested her blood and frowned. "That's weird, I'm totally fine."

Crystal and Joanna glanced at each other, and then Joanna asked, "Have you tested your blood lately, Max?"

"Not in a few hours," I said. I pulled out my glucose meter and pricked my finger. "Wow, this is crazy. I'm low."

We all stared at the dog, who was just looking up at me with her deep brown eyes. I knew right then and there that a DAD was going to be an amazing help.

There was still a long process ahead, though. The training period for a service dog was over two years, and it wasn't until January of my last year in London that I received the news from Crystal that I'd been waiting so long to hear.

"Max, I have the right dog for you, and he will be perfect for your lifestyle," she said. "His name is Orion, and I would like to bring him to meet you in London."

I was beyond excited, but I warned Crystal, "You're coming from

California. It's freezing here, and we have tons of snow. Will he be okay?"

"He should be fine," Crystal said. "What's more important is how the two of you get along."

The organization took great care in making sure the dog and person were the right match for one another. So I understood why it was so important that Crystal come to visit with Orion so we could meet. Orion was almost two, and he had completed all of his public access training and scent work. Now I just hoped that we'd have the right personality fit.

Luckily, I had nothing to worry about. I fell in love with Orion instantly! We did some basic training that weekend, which flew by. It was hard saying goodbye to him a few days later, knowing that it would still be another six months before he was mine. I was already looking forward to the additional training we'd be doing that summer in California, after which I'd finally be able to take Orion home.

Once Orion and I were reunited and he started living with me permanently, I quickly learned that he was so much more than just a DAD. In public, Orion is a much different dog than he is at home. When we're in public, Orion is all business—he's entirely focused on the task at hand. As a service dog, he has to wear a vest, which allows him to go with me anywhere. When he's at home, Orion doesn't wear a vest, but he's still working. That being said, if the time is right and I give him the green light to play, he's the same as any other dog.

It was that second role that made Orion so important to me during my early struggles that season. Although Orion was vital to me as a help for my diabetes, that season he was just as valuable to me as an emotional support.

Everyone says that a dog is man's best friend, but you don't realize how true that is until you have one. I would have loved to have had Orion with me all the time, but having to pack for and take care of a dog while we were on the road just wasn't possible—it wouldn't have been easy for either one of us. Luckily, I had great support. My family helped out, and I had a special dog-sitter named Tiffany, whom I relied on. And a few times during the season, when I was heading out on a ten-day road trip, Crystal would fly or drive to Arizona to pick up Orion and take him back to California, where he'd brush up on his training. Having a service dog was an incredible privilege, and it came with a huge responsibility, so I was very grateful for the support everyone provided.

I always looked forward to coming home after a road trip so that I could see Orion again. He was my family—the moment I saw him, he'd take my mind off of the frustrations of a rough game or a long trip. I often talked about it with other guys on the team who owned dogs. They all said the same thing: No matter what's going on or how pissed off you are, your dog always looks at you the same way.

I needed that support, because the season didn't get any easier. In December 2016, we were playing the Calgary Flames. With just a few seconds left in the second period and the game tied, Garnet Hathaway of the Flames and I got into a fight. Hathaway is a tough guy, and we were both just throwing as many punches as we could as hard as we could. When the dust settled, I came away with a cut above my eye and a broken thumb.

It was my first major injury. I needed surgery to repair the damage, which meant three months off the ice—I wouldn't get back until February 2017. I was so angry with myself. There was no way I could help my team when I was injured.

More than that, I knew that I could have prevented the injury. Normally, it takes a lot for me to get mad, but when my blood sugar is high, it doesn't take much. The night I broke my thumb, my blood sugar had been high. That's not to say that every time I fight, my blood sugar level is high. But at times like that, the reality is that I have a short fuse. I had known I was high that night, but I hadn't managed to deal with it. It wasn't an excuse for my actions, but knowing that I could have avoided being injured for months on end was tough to swallow. It was a huge learning experience, and a mistake I told myself I would never make again.

My parents and sisters tried to keep my spirits up during my rehab and recovery. It helped a bit—a simple text message from my mom about a movie she saw or something in the news always reminded me that there was a world outside of hockey. Sometimes, if she was with my little cousin, Devan, who was just a couple of years old, she would FaceTime me. Just seeing his smile always brightened my day. A few minutes of family time each day made a world of difference. I also took the time to work on myself and tried to strengthen my body and mind in order to make the most of a difficult situation.

When I finally got back on the ice, it took me a while to get back into game shape. On March 2, 2017—my birthday, no less—we were playing the Sabres, and during the second period I went really, really low. I had given myself too much insulin earlier in the day, and by the time the second period came around I was crashing.

At first I just felt tired. I figured I was still getting my legs back after my injury. Then it hit me that I was getting low. When I got on the ice, it felt like I was playing with a marble—I couldn't keep the puck on my stick. As soon as I took two hard strides, I was absolutely exhausted. I kept the rest of my shift simple—anytime I had the puck, I just chipped it out, something that I had never done before. The shift felt like it was a minute long, but in reality it was only fifteen or twenty seconds. That's when I said to myself, *Holy smokes, this is not safe.*

I knew I was low, but I didn't want to scare the trainers. When I got to the bench, I quietly told them that I was going low.

I had never missed a shift in the NHL because of my diabetes, but that night in Buffalo was about as close as it got.

"Can you pass me my drink?" I asked one of them. They passed me a special concoction that JP Major, one of the Coyotes trainers and strength coaches, had developed with Anne Peters. It was a specialty drink tailored to my needs. It was a blend of dextrose, a fast-burning carb to bring my blood glucose up; palatinose, otherwise known as isomaltulose, a slower-burning carb to maintain my blood sugar; and Gatorade powder, to add flavor and aid with an initial blood glucose spike. We often referred to it as "Max's Secret Stuff," in reference to the drink that Michael Jordan and the Looney Toons had in *Space Jam.*

Thankfully, there was a TV time-out coming up. While I was sitting there on the bench during the break, I was still a little dazed as my blood sugar slowly climbed back up. I was so out of it that I let my eyes wander into the stands. Suddenly I spotted a familiar face—my uncle Dash was sitting just a couple of rows behind the penalty boxes.

Great, now I'm hallucinating, I thought. But as my mind cleared, I realized that Dash was actually there. I started laughing to myself—the arena was sold out, my mind was foggy from my low blood sugar, and somehow I still managed to find my family in the crowd.

Right away I started feeling better. I finished the rest of my drink, the TV time-out ended, and I was back to normal on my next shift. After the period ended, I went straight to the table of food in the dressing room—the drink had bought me some time, but I needed real food if I was going to keep my blood sugar from crashing again. The trainers stared at me for a few seconds and then started laughing.

"Max, slow down," one of them said.

"I'll be fine," I said, my mouth full of banana.

The lifestyle of playing in the NHL pushes the boundary of living with type 1 diabetes. Exercise can cause blood sugar levels to drop, but it's not an exact science—you can't predict exactly how much your level will drop, whether it will be the same every time, or if it will happen during or after the exercise.

I finished the game that night, but the effects of going so low took their toll on me, and I didn't feel very well even a day later. We were playing back-to-back games, though, and the next day we were in Carolina. At that point in the NHL season everyone across the league feels the grind and is dealing with their own injuries. What makes you an NHL player is your ability to withstand the pain and find a way to mentally overcome those challenges.

You can always rely on your family when things get tough. Especially when it came to my dad. He'd lived it—the highs and lows of life in the NHL—and he knew how to guide me through it. He was always happy to help, but most of the time he let me come to him. He didn't want to distract me from the games. Sometimes he wouldn't even tell me beforehand if he was going to be at one. The only time I ever spotted him in the crowd was when I saw him in the stands in Chicago toward the end of the season.

I was setting up for a draw in the offensive zone at the end of a TV time-out, and I happened to see him a dozen rows up on the same side as the benches. I was surprised to see him there— whenever he went to a game, he sat much higher up or in a box so that I wouldn't accidentally spot him. I knew that if my dad caught me looking at him while I was on the ice, he'd never let me forget it, so I quickly brought my attention back to the play. Later, when I was back on the bench, I told myself I wouldn't look over at him again during the game. I hated knowing where he was—it was such a distraction—but I managed to stay locked in on the play. I never told him that I saw him sitting there. He would have been mad at me if I had.

"Don't think about the crowd," he was always telling me. "Nothing matters other than what's happening on the ice."

I called my dad a lot toward the end of my second season. Because of my hand injury, I ended up playing only fifty-nine games that year. Even worse, we missed the playoffs again.

I hated missing the playoffs but I really liked the core of young players we had in Arizona. As much as I wanted to win and be in the playoffs, I knew from my dad how hard it is to be a winner in the NHL. As long as we kept working together, I figured we'd start moving in the right direction.

I went into the summer of 2017 determined to get into the best shape of my life so that I could turn things around the next year. But a few months into my off-season, I had another scary incident.

I had recently switched from an insulin pump to insulin pen injections. My insulin pump looked a bit like an older generation iPod. It would clip onto my waist and hold a reservoir of insulin that lasted three days. That unit was then connected by a tube to a site, a little patch that looked like a Band-Aid and adhered to either my butt cheek or my stomach. The unit delivered short-acting insulin twenty-four hours a day. There was a basal setting—a drip that was automatically administered throughout the twenty-four hours—as well as a bolus setting, which I manually dialed in at each meal. The pump used the same type of insulin for both settings. The pump was supposed to be convenient and easy, but it had become too much of a hassle for me. Things like my sweat, the friction from my equipment, or the force from a body check could sometimes break the pump or throw off the tubing or the site. I found myself often having to clean up the mess that came with having a pump, which just led to more stress as I chased my blood sugar levels far too often.

So, I went back to pen injections, which were a more burdensome process. I used two types of pens. And unlike the pump, each pen held a different type of insulin. One was a long-acting insulin, which effectively did the same thing as the basal setting on the pump. The other pen held short-acting insulin, so it functioned the same way as the pump's bolus setting. At the end of each pen, there was a dial to adjust the amount of my insulin dose. Because the two types of insulin worked differently, they required two completely different dosages. I usually gave myself forty units of the long-acting insulin every morning and about five to eight units of insulin before every meal. I knew that with the pens, every time I injected myself, I could control exactly how much insulin was going into my system, and I could guarantee that it would be delivered. In general, people with diabetes have the same control with pumps as they do with shots—it all depends on the person to give the insulin correctly.

But one day, I was at the house of my girlfriend for a family dinner. It was a long, two-and-a-half-hour meal, and I got distracted with all of the food and conversation. We were talking and hanging out afterward, when I excused myself and headed downstairs— I needed to inject myself with some insulin to balance out the carbs I had just eaten.

My first mistake had been not testing my blood and giving myself insulin before the meal. I checked my blood and saw that I was pretty high. I could feel it—my mouth was dry, I was irritable, and my mind was all over the place. I reached into my diabetes bag and grabbed the pen with my short-acting insulin—the one I always used for meals.

I had the right insulin. But because I was distracted and the pen was the same thickness as my long-acting one, I dialed up the dosage to the usual long-acting insulin level. Then, without thinking any more of it, I injected the insulin into my butt cheek.

As I did, I was talking to my girlfriend, who was outside the bedroom door. Just as I was about to pull out the needle, I looked back. I was shocked to see that I had dialed up my short-acting insulin way too high. In fact, way too high didn't do it justice—I'd given myself over thirty units of short-acting insulin, when all I needed was five!

Within three seconds of realizing what I had just done, it hit me that I was in serious trouble.

I took a couple of deep breaths and tried to figure out a plan. I knew I had a bit of time before the insulin hit me. First things first, I had to decide whether or not to call 911. That much short-acting insulin could kill a person.

Luckily, my blood sugar was already high; it was at fifteen because I had waited so long after eating to inject myself with the insulin.

"Can you get me some apple juice, please?" I asked my girlfriend.

She could tell right away that something was wrong. She brought me a juice bottle, and I sat down on the couch and chugged it down.

"Can I please have more?" I asked. "A lot more."

At that point, my girlfriend could tell something was seriously wrong. I could see she was scared.

"Please do not panic," I said to her. "I need to stay calm. If I'm not calm, my blood sugar level is going to plummet."

I kept drinking as much juice as possible while I called Anne Peters. Anne had become something of a second mom to me, and she was always calm under pressure.

"Max, this is unexpected," she said when she picked up.

"Anne, I've really screwed up," I said.

"What's wrong?" she asked.

I filled her in on what had happened.

"That's not good," she said when I told her how much insulin I'd injected. "Did you call 911?"

"Not yet," I said.

"If you vomit or you begin to pass out, you have to call 911 so that the paramedics can get you to the hospital immediately. For now, you need to eat as many long-acting carbs as you can. You're also going to need a shot of glucagon," she said, referring to the same type of injection that the Tookes had given me when I'd gone low and unresponsive when I was their billet.

My glucagon was at home, so I ended my call with Anne and dialed my mom.

"Mom, I'm coming home," I said.

"What happened?" she asked.

"I injected myself with way too much insulin. I need as many different types of carbohydrates and glucose as possible."

"I'll get it ready. Get here safely."

When I walked in the door to my mom's place, I felt the insulin beginning to hit me, and it was hitting me hard. I knew I had to stay calm, otherwise it would only make things worse. My blood sugar level was crashing. I started guzzling juice while my mom called Anne to update her.

I had just eaten an entire dinner at my girlfriend's family's house—a massive steak with sweet potato fries, salad, vegetables, and then two gluten-free cookies topped off with some berries. I had been completely stuffed, but I knew that I needed an insane amount of carbs to counter the overdose of insulin that I'd accidentally given myself. There was no way to get the insulin out once I'd put it in, so it was a race between the insulin taking effect and the sugar I was ingesting getting into my bloodstream to counter it. Somehow my stomach found a way to make the room that I needed at that moment.

I crushed orange juice and apple juice. I had chocolate cake and pasta. I followed that up with chocolate almond milk and a slice of toast with peanut butter and jam. I ate and drank all of that within an hour of getting home.

At the same time, my mom was getting the glucagon needle ready. No matter how much I ate and drank, there was a chance it wouldn't be enough sugar to counteract the insulin, so we wanted to be ready. We were managing an emergency situation, and we wanted to be as safe as possible as we tried to avert the worst possible scenario.

Not many people ever give themselves a shot of glucagon. Usually, by the time it's needed, the person with diabetes is unresponsive and unable to give the shot to themselves. And even if they were, glucagon shots are no fun—they hurt, they often make you vomit, and they're only supposed to be used as a last resort.

I kept eating and eating—ice cream, honey, maple syrup, cereal, any sugar or carbohydrate we had on hand. The entire kitchen counter was covered with food. While I ate, my mom timed the intervals between each blood test with the glucose meter, and she recorded a reading every five minutes—if I had to go to the hospital, she wanted to be able to give them my exact readings. My sisters were there, too, ready to call 911 if needed. I hoped I could eat enough to keep from passing out. I could barely choke down the food as I focused on not being sick. If I was, it would have been a disaster—my body wouldn't be able to digest anything or absorb the sugar from the food, and I would have to go to the hospital immediately. At one point, my numbers plunged and we were ready to call the paramedics, but a few minutes later, they slowly started to climb, and I began to feel a little bit better.

I didn't get to sleep until the sun was almost up. I kept feeding sugar into my system, and my mom kept monitoring my blood sugar levels. The next afternoon, I came downstairs and sat beside my mom in the kitchen.

"You don't look great," she said, giving me a hug.

"Do you think I should work out today?" I asked.

"Max, are you crazy?" she said. "Absolutely not."

"Okay, how about if I try to skate tonight, at least?"

"No, Max. You were lucky. Hopefully there is never going to be a next time like this. But if there is, please just go straight to the hospital," my mom pleaded.

"I promise," I said.

I slowly recovered over the next couple of days. I was grumpy and tired—it felt like I'd run a marathon and was recovering—but at least my blood sugar levels held steady.

I couldn't believe I'd make a mistake like that. I had been living with the disease for a decade—surely I should have known better? I had made injection mistakes before, but nothing ever that bad.

I was always in the moment, but I was also a forgetful person. It's one thing to forget your jersey when you're packing your hockey bag as a kid. But when it comes to health, those sorts of mistakes are the kind of thing you can't afford to let happen. I'd let my guard down, and I realized what a huge mistake I'd made. I could have killed myself with that injection screwup if I hadn't had help. Once again, my family had my back.

My blood sugar levels were a little harder to read for the next few weeks, too. Later that summer, I was hanging out with my sisters at home. My mom was out getting groceries, so we decided to order a pizza.

"What kind of pizza do you want, Max?" Carlin asked.

"I don't want pizza," I snapped, looking down at my phone.

Carlin and Avery exchanged a look that I didn't see. They could already tell what I was too distracted to know—I was snapping at people, which meant I was going low.

Carlin knew that I was hungry and needed to eat something, so she ordered anyway. A few minutes later, everyone heard a massive bang. That bang was me; I had fallen trying to walk up the stairs.

I had realized I was going low, so I was on my way to get some juice from the fridge when I wiped out. I got up and somehow made it to the fridge, hoping to get some ice cream. That's when I fell again.

Carlin came running over and found me sitting by the fridge, my head bleeding. She calmly started talking to me to see how I was feeling, and then Avery came running. Carlin got me sitting upright and had me hold a towel to the cut on my head. Then she gave me the ice cream that I was trying to get in the first place.

"Thanks," I slurred.

I was conscious, but not totally with it at that point. As I started to eat some ice cream, I slowly started to come out of it and become more normal. Five minutes later, it really hit me how low I'd been. I was thankful that my sisters were so smart and calm.

"Thank you both so much," I said to Carlin and Avery later that night, once I'd recovered a bit. "I don't know what I'd do without you."

By the end of the summer, I had fully recovered. I was ready to put the past year behind me. The season had been a tough one, and the summer had thrown a lot at me. Once again, it was determination, resilience, and my support network of friends and family that had carried me through the tough times. All year long, my priorities had been out of whack. I'd lost sight of what was most important to me: managing my diabetes.

My health had always been my priority, but those two incidents were a wake-up call, and they put things in perspective for me. I could see that I'd been playing with fire more than I should have. As a person with type 1 diabetes, one mistake can potentially cost you your life. Everyone makes mistakes—it's impossible not to. It's moments like those when you rely on the team around you for support. There's no shame in asking for help. I realized that, no matter how prepared I thought I was—I could be a professional athlete, I could manage my condition—it didn't matter; I was still learning from my mistakes on a daily basis. I was lucky. Lucky that I'd had help when I needed it. Lucky that I had such incredible support around me to help me when I made a mistake. I was grateful for that, and it was a reality check. But now it was time for me to get back on track.

10

PUSH YOUR LIMITS

Before the start of the 2017–18 season, my third in the NHL, the Coyotes decided to make a few changes. The NHL is a business, and every year teams across the league make tough decisions. One of the toughest was the team's decision to part ways with Shane Doan.

When Shane was released from the Coyotes, I called him to thank him for everything he had done for me my first two years in the league. Doan always knew what he had to do as a leader, and he made everyone around him feel comfortable. He was down-to-earth and humble, and he led by example. He was always willing to let others talk, but when he spoke, everyone listened. I looked up to Shane for so many reasons that went beyond the rink, from how much he valued his family to what he gave back to his community. I considered myself lucky to play alongside a legend like Shane, and words alone weren't enough to thank him.

I tried not to let the changes get to me. Going into that third season, my mind-set was totally different. I had a level of comfort and confidence that I hadn't had in any season before. My focus wasn't so much on how I would prove myself. I had a new challenge, one I was completely dedicated to: helping the Coyotes make the playoffs. The difficulties of the past season were behind me now. I was back on track and looking to put everything on the line.

By the time I got back to Arizona, I was gearing up and ready to hit the ground running. But there was one thing in my way: traffic. Not a mental jam, but literal car traffic. The 101 loop from North Scottsdale to Glendale was often locked with bumper-to-bumper traffic.

I always drove to games, and by the time I got there, my stress levels would be through the roof. I was monitoring my blood sugar levels really closely after what had happened in the summer, and I was still experimenting with different solutions for diabetes management, hoping something would stick. My doctors and I discovered that the stress of driving to the rink through that traffic was causing my blood sugar levels to spike. When I got to the rink, my blood sugar would be high from the stress and adrenaline, so I would give myself short-acting insulin to bring it down. At that point, my blood sugar levels weren't stable, and the last time I wanted to be out of whack and chasing my blood sugar like that was when I was trying to get ready for a game.

So before the start of my third season, I came up with the idea of hiring a car service to drive to me to home games. It would be another investment, but I hoped it would help me, and I was fortunate to be in a position where I could make that choice. I took the plan to the Coyotes trainers, and they agreed.

It worked. Not having to drive eliminated all of that stress, and I was able to arrive at the rink feeling more relaxed and with my blood sugar far more stable.

My diabetes support group now went far beyond just the Coyotes training staff. I also had my family, Orion, and my teammates for my day-to-day support. And I was fortunate to have the help of some of the best specialists in the world.

I still consulted with Anne on a regular basis, too. I spoke to her every two weeks at the very least. Usually it was more like once a week. I'd call her if I had any questions about my diabetes or if I read about any new technology that was on the market.

I had finally accepted the fact that I didn't have as much control over my blood sugar levels as I thought I did. I realized that, if I didn't figure it out, I wouldn't have a long career in the NHL. I was trying to do everything and anything to get this right. Anne and I reviewed new, different types of insulin, continuous glucose monitors, and my diets to determine what worked best, and we sent videos and articles back and forth about new breakthroughs in diabetes research. We'd make a small change, give it time to see how my body reacted, and then adapt from there.

It was amazing to me that, even though I'd lived with diabetes much of my life, I was still learning more every day. Today, there are more ways than ever for people with type 1 diabetes to manage their disease and enjoy long, fulfilled lives in which they survive and thrive. I know my own body better than anyone, and I recognize that the challenges I face are different from what other people might experience—some people with diabetes might never even have the sorts of hypoglycemic episodes that I've had. So I'm constantly reading up on the disease and studying it to figure out what works best for me. There is so much I can still learn about insulin and why my body reacts to it the way it does. How do different injection methods affect the way my body absorbs the insulin? How did I sleep the night before and did that affect my blood sugar? What improved tools—new forms of glucagon, nasal spray, low-dose injections with smaller needles—will roll out as technology improves? In my opinion, Anne is one of the best diabetes specialists in the world, and even an expert like her is still learning.

Routine and discipline were always going to be part of the equation for my diabetes management. But my routines were changing that year. Just before the start of the season, the Coyotes hired a whole new training staff. It was hard seeing the old staff go—they had been such an instrumental part of my journey in the NHL so far. When the new staff arrived, one of the first things we did was sit down so that I could tell them all about my diabetes, how I managed it, and what I would need from them.

"From what I hear, you test your blood a lot," one trainer said.

"I do," I said with a laugh. "Although I don't test at the ten-minute mark anymore because I'm more dialed in. I'll still need you to have my supplies on the bench, and I'll look to you when I need them."

When I was finished, the trainers glanced at each other, and then the head trainer, Dave Zenobi, nodded. "I'm impressed. You seem to know what you're doing. Keep doing your thing, and know that whatever you need us to do, we're always here for you."

I was thankful that they trusted me to manage my own diabetes. I knew I could trust them to help me if anything ever went wrong, and I appreciated the fact that it was a two-way street. It was finally starting to feel as though I was controlling my disease instead of the other way around. I felt a newfound sense of independence.

The next thing that Anne and I decided to focus on was my nutrition plan. Food is all-important for people with type 1 diabetes. Everything we eat needs to be for a reason, and it has to be calculated. My constant snacking wasn't working so well with our hockey schedule.

"You need to give your body time to break down all of those simple and complex carbohydrates from meals," Anne told me.

I had to completely rethink my diet. Instead of my snacking throughout the day, Anne suggested I eat three or four meals, and nothing more. So I hired a personal chef named Ian to come help me out during the season. Ian had studied under my last chef, Johnny, and his wife, Whitney, whom I had worked with during my first two years in Arizona. My diabetes team was growing ever larger, and having a personal chef help me with my nutrition was just another part of my personal diabetes toolkit. It was an investment in my body—one I was lucky enough to be able to make—and I knew it would eliminate a lot of variables and guesswork when it came to my blood sugar levels. Not all of them, of course—the variables for a person with type 1 diabetes are endless—but enough so that when I showed up to the rink, all I would have to think about was hockey.

Ian was a young guy and a professional chef, but he quickly realized that cooking for a person with type 1 diabetes was a lot harder than it first seemed. After a couple of weeks, I found Ian in the kitchen and asked how things were going.

"Honestly, man," he said as he cut up a chicken breast, "I think I'm going to have to re-teach myself how to cook."

And he did. Ian became a diabetes specialist in his own right. He read books about the disease and diet to see how they related, and he talked regularly with Anne and her team. Working with Anne changed everything when it came to my nutrition. Ian and I monitored my blood sugar levels throughout the day and the meals I ate. We recorded how well I slept, how many hours of sleep I got, how much I weighed, how many grams of carbohydrates I ate at a meal, how much insulin I'd injected before the meal, and anything else that could be used to monitor my diabetes. Then we sent every bit of data to Anne and her dietician so that they could refine the plan.

One day, after dinner, we decided to shoot some pool. That sounds simple enough. We were in the middle of the game, joking around and having a good time, when Ian gave me a funny look.

"Are you all right?" he asked.

I was lining up for a shot, but I couldn't focus on the ball. I looked up at Ian with a glassy-eyed stare. I knew I was going low.

"I think I should test my blood," I said slowly.

"Definitely," he said. "Why don't you sit down."

I pricked my finger and then looked at the number on my glucose meter—1.4, which is insanely low. All of a sudden I had blurred vision and could barely see straight. Ian grabbed me a bunch of apple juice. I finished it quickly, and started to rebound. Before long, I was feeling much more like myself.

For me, the incident wasn't all that unique. I'd known something was wrong and managed to quickly fix it. But it was an eye-opener for Ian, who'd never seen me go that low, that fast before.

I'm the sort of guy who always wants to keep fighting. That's a great personality trait to have if you play in the NHL. If we're down 5–1, I'm not giving up—every shift, I'm going to try and score to get us back into the game. But when I get low and that same voice inside my head tells me, *You can get through this*, it can be dangerous. When I was younger, I was more willing to listen to that voice and try to shrug things off. But more and more, I was learning that sometimes you have to know your limits.

Luckily, I had a coach who also understood that. Rick Tocchet had been hired as our new head coach at the start of the season. I saw a lot of my dad in Rick. He genuinely cared about everyone, and he connected with you immediately. He was an old-school guy—as long as you showed up to the rink, worked your hardest every single day, and bought into what the team was trying to do, Rick would have your back no matter what. He wanted to win just as bad as, if not more than, every guy in our locker room.

Toward the end of the year, we were in Minnesota for a game. Before our morning skate, Tocchet pulled me into the visitor's equipment room.

I expected him to chew me out. Rick doesn't play head games—he says what he means, and he'll call you out when he needs to. I respected that about him. I had been fighting a cold, which always drives my blood sugar system into chaos. When my body is fighting an illness, my blood sugar levels run high and my body is resistant to the insulin, so depending on how sick I am, I have to increase my insulin dosages by anywhere from 10 to 25 percent.

"Everything good?" Rick asked.

I froze. It wasn't the question I was expecting.

"Yeah, I'm all good," I said.

"No, you're not," he replied. "What's up?"

"I didn't play well last game," I said. "That's on me."

Tocchet paused. "Max, I didn't call you here to talk about your play last game. What I want to know is whether there's anything I can do differently to help you."

I was blown away. "You, the trainers, and the team already do so much for me," I said. "I'm thankful for everything you guys do."

"I don't want you to ever feel that you are asking for too much from us," he said. "Whatever you're dealing with, I want to help. But you need to communicate with me and the rest of the staff."

I instantly felt a huge weight lift off my shoulders; I could breathe again. It was one of the first one-on-one conversations I'd had with Tocchet, and I could see that he was a good person, and he genuinely cared about his players.

"I will, I promise," I said. "All I want is to help this team win."

"If the game's not going your way, you have to simplify and not do too much."

Tocchet wasn't just talking about playing with diabetes—he was talking about the difficulties that come with the daily grind and the ups and downs of the NHL, things that every player in the league battles.

"I'll level with you, Max," Tocchet said. "I'll be straight up with you, and I'll tell you if you make a mistake. But it's all just to make you a better player."

I left feeling so much better than I did when I went in. Tocchet was one of the most respected guys in the league, both as a player and as a coach, and at that moment, a light bulb went off. It was the first time I felt I could talk openly and be heard like that without being judged. Tocchet had given me a safe place to talk, and he'd given me my confidence back—I trusted he wanted to see me succeed. I'd been lucky to have incredible coaches throughout my career, but I'd never been able to connect with a coach like that. It was a breakthrough, and I knew I would carry that lesson with me going forward.

My attitude was tested more than once throughout the rest of that season. We were struggling to win games, and I couldn't seem to put the puck in the net. Each game that passed without a point for me or the team, I lost a little more confidence. And when you lose confidence, everything else in your game goes to shit.

I had never experienced a drought like that. Like anyone else,

I had ups and downs during a season. But I'd never had one that was this bad or that went on for this long. Hockey wasn't fun anymore, and it felt as though there wasn't anything I could do to stop the slide. The more I thought about the problem, the more I stressed about it. And that stress threw my blood sugar out of whack, which meant I went through unpredictable mood swings. Everything was off.

Ironically, the only time that I was able to calm myself down and be productive was when I stopped thinking about hockey. When I stepped back, took a breath, and relaxed away from the rink, it changed everything. It was eye-opening—I realized that playing in the NHL had started as my passion and my job, but I was letting it consume my life.

I had thought that life in the NHL was all there was, and I'd forgotten about the other things that had a big impact on my life—family, friends, Orion, having fun. Hockey didn't exist apart from those things. They were all a part of my life and I couldn't have one without the other.

I talked to a few people about what was happening to me, including a sports psychologist. Doing that allowed me to better understand what was going on in my life and chart a way through all the chaos. I made more time for myself and sought out more quiet moments at home with Orion. I tried to reflect on what was going on inside me and what was making me feel that way.

I also relied on the help of the team around me. Once again, Rick Tocchet's guidance and support made the difference—I don't know what I would have done without him.

One day, we were in Minnesota preparing for a game that night. I was getting ready for our morning skate when Rick called me into the equipment room for a meeting.

"I want you to do one thing tonight," Rick began. "Go have fun. Just play and don't worry about anything else."

"I feel bad," I admitted. "I still haven't shown you what I can do."

I had so much respect for Rick. He had coached some of the best players in the world, and he had won it all as both a player and a coach. I didn't want to be a burden on the team. But Rick and I talked for a while, and he made it clear that he was cheering me on and wanted nothing but the best. He knew what I was capable of on the ice.

I didn't realize how long we were talking until I finally headed back to the dressing room and found that everyone was already on the ice.

Rick's words were like the ultimate motivational speech. Finally, I felt that I was in a better space. I told myself that I wasn't going to dwell on the past or what had happened earlier in the year. I had to make those last few months of the season count.

It seemed to work. Our team won eleven games down the stretch—not enough to make the playoffs, but it felt good to finally be clicking. Personally, I felt good on and off the ice, too, which was a relief. All of the trials and errors of the past few years—both the ones on the ice and the ones related to my diabetes management—were finally paying off. For the first time in my life, I felt as though I finally had everything under control.

I hoped we could pick up the same momentum at the start of the next season. During my end-of-season exit interviews, Rick Tocchet once again told me something that comforted me and made me feel better.

"You can't have a career in the NHL and not go through a season like you just did," he said. "The ups and downs that you went through are part of life in the NHL. It is what it is. And I am proud of the way that you overcame that adversity."

As far as I was concerned, I was a Coyote, and I planned to be back the next year so I could give the team everything I had. I believed in myself and in what our team could do.

In June 2018, shortly after the season ended, I went to New York City to spend some time with my dad. We were visiting with an old family friend when my phone rang.

"Hello?" I said.

"Max, it's John." It was John Chayka, the Coyotes' GM. He was calling to let me know that I had been traded to the Montreal Canadiens.

I was in a daze, but I managed to pull myself together. "Thank you for everything, John," I said. "I've loved being a Coyote. I wish you and the rest of the organization nothing but the best."

Almost the second after I hung up, the phone rang again. This time it was Montreal's GM, Marc Bergevin.

"I wanted to call and personally welcome you to the Canadiens," Marc said. We talked a little about how excited we were for the upcoming season, and just like that, I was a Canadien.

I shared the news with my dad and our friend, and they both gave me a huge hug. I couldn't stop smiling at the thought of playing in a heritage market like Montreal, but still, the moment felt bittersweet. I really wanted to be a part of the team the Coyotes were building in the desert and to win with my first team in the NHL. I had built some strong friendships there—some of the younger guys on the team felt like family. But I knew that I'd have those friendships my entire life, no matter where I played, so I told myself to focus on the positives.

I had one other concern, though. I'd worn number 16 ever since I was a kid, but that wasn't going to be an option anymore. Number 16 had been retired in Montreal in honour of Henri Richard. I had some other numbers in mind, but one of them stood out: 13. Mats Sundin's number. Luckily, it hadn't been retired, and when I saw that, I knew what I'd be wearing when I pulled on my Canadiens jersey in the fall.

With the trade finalized, there was only one thing for me to do: go out and show Montreal that they had made the right move. My goal over the summer was to tap into a whole new energy system. I had my blood sugar dialed in thanks to the changes I'd made the last season, but one thing I was still struggling with was my engine—I wanted to be able to play more, be more efficient, and not get as tired.

I needed to find a whole other gear, one where I could chase down the puck in the third period with two minutes to go and still have the energy to split the D and hold off a defenseman while going to the net. If I could find those new levels of energy, my brain wouldn't be focused on fatigue. Instead, it would be free to perform the way I needed it to and recognize whether I needed to go to my backhand or my forehand in the situation.

I reached out to Mats Sundin and pestered him with questions about training and conditioning—I'd never forgotten the sight of him on the stationary bike after a game. We caught up early that summer, before I started my training, and he explained what sort of fitness he thought I needed to get my game to the next level. Mats shared with me the sorts of workouts he had done, and suggested I try some of them.

Not long after, I started working with former Canadian Olympian and track star Mark McKoy. I remember one of the first workouts from Mats that we did. I ran 500 meters, then rested for exactly one minute and thirty seconds. Then I ran 1,000 meters and rested for exactly two minutes. Then another 500 meters with a minute and a half of rest, followed by 1,000 meters and two minutes rest, and then a final 500 meters.

On paper, the workout didn't look that bad. The first time I tried it, though, I was humbled. To do the workout properly, I had to stick to the exact rest times between runs. But, I couldn't do it—halfway through, I could barely breathe.

I didn't give up, though. I had always wanted to be like Mats, one of the all-time greats. We were different players with different body types, but I still held myself to his standard. I kept working away and pushing myself, and bit by bit, what seemed impossible on the track or on the ice became a little more possible.

By the end of August, I felt better on the ice than I had ever felt before the start of camp. A lot of that was thanks to the doctors and trainers I was working with. But I also felt more grounded than I had before. I had spent as much time over the summer working on my personal issues as I had on my body. I was still finding those quiet, meditative moments, either by myself or with Orion and my family, that helped me remain calm and balanced.

After I was traded, some people asked me if I was worried about playing in Montreal. "Isn't there a lot of pressure?" they asked. Each time I heard the questions, I laughed and shook my head. Worried was the last thing I was feeling.

"Playing in a place like Montreal is why I play the game," I'd respond.

There were some things I knew I'd have to work on. For one, I didn't speak French. I'd learned some French as a kid, but I was never that great at it. When I moved to Montreal, I wished I remembered more of the language. I had a new chef, Emileigh, helping me with my nutrition, and I asked her what I should learn to say. *"Je vais manger des spaghettis"*—"I'm going to eat spaghetti," she said with a grin.

But when it came to hockey, I always loved playing in front of big crowds—the bigger the better. I wanted the pressure and the sold-out stands. I wanted to walk down the street and meet people who knew the game and knew what was going on with the team. I loved the fact that, in Montreal, hockey was a religion. I didn't see playing for the Canadiens as pressure—I saw it as a privilege and an opportunity to prove myself and represent something special.

The first time I walked into the Canadiens' practice facility, I took a moment to check out the names of all the Hall-of-Famers on the wall around me—Maurice Richard, Guy Lafleur, Jean Béliveau. *Legends*, I thought. *And I'm lucky enough to wear the same jersey as them.* My new life as a member of the Montreal Canadiens sunk in, and I couldn't wait to get started. All I needed to do was play hard every shift and enjoy myself. If I did that, I was confident I could live up to all those players who wore the sweater before me.

Despite what some people predicted about our team in the preseason, we knew as players what we were capable of and what we could accomplish. Our goal entering the season was to surprise as many teams as possible.

We started the season with a big test against the Toronto Maple Leafs. I had been looking forward to that first game for so long. In the summer, while I was training, I'd had the date circled in my calendar, thinking about how much fun it would be. The days leading up to that opening game were a big emotional roller coaster. There were moments where the nerves kicked in and I psyched myself out a little. But then I'd see my teammates on the ice, and I'd feel as though nothing could stop us.

The game was nonstop back-and-forth. We struck first halfway through the first period. I was standing right in front of the net when Artturi Lehkonen swung up from behind the goal line and fired the puck in the short side. I threw my arms up in the air and raced over to congratulate him. I could hear cheers and boos from the crowd, but I didn't care. We were on the board and ready to keep things rolling.

The Leafs pulled ahead 2–1, but I earned my second assist of the night when we managed to tie it up on the power play in the second period.

We ended up losing the game in overtime, but I honestly felt as though we were the better team in the game, and the way we played that night gave us the confidence to start the year with the right mind-set.

A few weeks later, we were back in Montreal to face the St. Louis Blues. During warm-up, I was skating around with Jonathan Drouin, and everything seemed to be clicking. The puck was whipping off our sticks, and our passes were connecting perfectly. We looked at each other and I just said, "We're feeling pretty good, eh?"

At the start of my first shift of the game, we were hemmed in our own zone for a little too long. We were grinding away, and I thought, *Oh no, it is going to be one of those nights against St. Louis.*

The next thing I knew, the puck went up the wall and was chipped out to me. I burst out of the zone and was off to the races. I was barreling down the right wing, skating as hard as I could, and I could feel Vladimir Tarasenko hot on my heels. I crossed the blue line on a two-on-one with Drouin on the left. I had next to no time to make a decision, so I threw a backhand on net. I tried to put it low on the far side so that Drouin could pick up the rebound. But my shot went along the ice, surprising Jake Allen and slipping into the back of the net.

The Bell Centre lit up and the crowd leapt to its feet with a roar as the horn sounded. I pumped my fist, and the biggest smile spread across my face as I skated through the celebration train at the bench. I hadn't been that fired up since I scored in the gold medal game of the World Juniors. Just like that, my total love for the game of hockey was back with me in full force.

A few weeks later, Mats and my dad came to see one of my games. I met up with them in the hallway afterward, where they greeted me with big smiles.

"That was the best I've ever seen you play in the NHL," Mats said.

"Thanks, Mats," I said with a grin.

Then Mats got serious. "You were making a lot of good plays out there," he said. "You just keep doing what you're doing—don't change a thing and don't get comfortable. Keep working toward being great. Do the work no one else is doing."

I took Mats's words to heart. As a person with diabetes, I didn't have a choice. There was always going to be work I had to do that no one else did. But I wasn't going to let that stop me. I was determined to never miss a shift and to always be ready when Coach Claude Julien called my name. I owed it to my teammates, to the family and friends who had helped me get to where I was, and to myself.

Every time I see my sweater hanging in my stall with the Canadiens logo on it, I feel like I'm living a dream. But it's one I never want to wake up from. It is the biggest honour I've ever had in my life.

AFTERWORD

In 2017, during a break from my training, I was invited to Washington, D.C., to be a part of a big event for JDRF. The event was called Children's Congress, and it brought together volunteers and staff from across the country to advocate for those living with type 1 diabetes. JDRF is the leading global organization funding type 1 diabetes research. The organization was trying to secure funding for the next few years of their special diabetes program.

I sat on a panel of people, all of whom had diabetes. There were some actors with me, such as Paul Sparks from *House of Cards*, and I saw Charlie Kimball, the IndyCar driver. Nicole Johnson, Miss America 1999, was part of the group, as were the CNN reporter Cristina Alesci and an amazing scientist named Dr. Aaron Kowalski, who at that time was chief mission officer for JDRF. *This is an impressive group*, I thought as I sat down at the table and took in everyone's faces. *Better bring my A-game.*

We talked to members of both the House of Representatives and the Senate to try and convince them to approve the necessary funding—roughly $150 million every two years. It was a long day, but a rewarding one. A series of experts made presentations of behalf of JDRF to ensure there wouldn't be a reduction or stoppage in the government funding. To highlight how important it was for the funding to continue, the experts revealed a startling fact: in the

United States, more people die from complications of type 1 and type 2 diabetes every year than from AIDS and breast cancer combined. The funding we were there to support would help save lives.

After the political presentation was out of the way, we had a chance to get to connect with people more personally. We left the government offices and went to a meeting room where 160 kids and their parents were waiting for us. The kids took turns asking questions, and we went around the group and added our two cents.

At one point, a kid addressed a question to me directly.

"Max, does Orion keep watch over you while you sleep?" she asked.

"Kind of," I said. "He sleeps at night, just like any other dog, but he's always sensitive to my blood sugar levels. If I go low in the middle of the night, he'll pick up the scent of my low blood sugar, and he'll wake me up so that I can fix it. It's especially helpful the nights after games."

I could see in the kid's face that she knew exactly what I was talking about, and I caught other people around the room nodding in agreement—we'd all been through a similar experience.

Sometimes, after doing a hockey interview or talking with media, I find myself drained. It can take a lot of focus to make sure I'm answering the questions properly. But when I left the diabetes event that day, I felt exactly the opposite—I was fired up.

On my worst days, I can feel like I'm the only person in the world struggling with diabetes. Events like the one JDRF held in Washington, D.C., remind me that I'm not alone. As soon as you have the opportunity to speak with another person with diabetes, whether they're eight years old or eighty, you form a special connection that no one else has.

I find that when I talk to a kid about the disease, I learn just as much from them as they might learn from me. I love hearing other people with type 1 diabetes talk about their experiences because then I can compare them to what I deal with all the time. That's how you learn—by talking to other people and listening. I compare it to hockey. For me, getting an assist and seeing someone else succeed is the best. I get more out of that than I do from scoring a goal myself. And just like I get a thrill out of setting up a teammate for a goal, I love talking to a young person with diabetes and trying to encourage and inspire them. Since that event in Washington, I have spoken to thousands of people living with type 1 diabetes. I feel it's an important job for me— to try and help kids and inspire them, just as Bobby Clarke did for me.

A few months later, after the season started, I was getting changed after a practice when our team media representative came up to me.

"Max," he said, "there's a young kid and his dad here to meet you."

I went out and introduced myself to the two of them. The boy had just been diagnosed with type 1 diabetes.

I didn't want to scare them, but I cautioned them they were about to go through a lot of ups and downs over the next few years.

"If you dig deep enough, though, you can get through it all," I said to the boy. "If you want to play in the NHL, you can play in the NHL."

The dad's eyes lit up. "That's exactly what he wants to do!" he said.

"If that's your dream, then go for it," I said to the boy as he smiled. "And if you or your dad have any questions for me, reach out to me anytime and I'm more than happy to help."

Shortly after I first made the NHL, when I was just starting to talk to other kids with diabetes, my mom said something that has stuck with me every single day.

"Your diabetes may feel like a burden, Max," she said. "But it is also a gift. You have an opportunity to truly make a difference in people's lives, and that's something that many people don't have the power to do. It's up to you to make the most of it."

Before every game, as the anthems play, I close my eyes and think on my mom's words and what they mean. For those few seconds, the rush and the pressure of the game all disappear, and I flash back to being a kid again. I see my mom waking up at six in the morning on a cold, dark Saturday to take me to practice. I see and smell the narrow hallway at Port Credit Arena in Mississauga. I see me and my sisters in the back of my dad's car as he drops us off for one of my Friday night games, my two yellow TPS sticks under my arm and my sisters' chatter around my head. Images of junior and international play rush past me as I reflect on all of the sacrifices my family and those close to me have made to allow me to achieve my dream of playing in the NHL.

Finally, when the anthems end, I give my head a shake and think about all of the kids who are trying to follow their dreams and how watching the game that night might inspire them. And then it's game on.

I play hockey because I love it. There's nothing I would rather do, and I look forward to each and every time I get to step on the ice. It's the greatest game in the world.

As a person with diabetes, I push the boundaries of the disease to the limits. I don't have the luxury of doing the same thing every single day, and my schedule and job add to what is already a tough everyday battle with the disease. Nothing is the same day to day, or even minute to minute. As a person with diabetes, you can plan, and calculate, and strategize, but even then, things can change and you have to adapt instantly. There's no such thing as being over-prepared. But my goal has been the same since the first skating lesson I took at two years old—I want to play in the NHL and I want to be the best player I can be. I want to help my team win championships and to play hockey at the highest level possible as long as I can.

Type 1 diabetes didn't stop me from fulfilling my lifelong dream of making the NHL—it doesn't have to stop anyone from following their dream. I will continue living with this disease twenty-four hours a day, seven days a week, for the rest of my life. There are risks that come with that, but there's no need to be scared of the disease. And even though I never get a day off because of my diabetes, I am still so excited about the journey ahead. Living with this disease has made me a stronger person and turned me into who I am. This is just the start, and diabetes hasn't stopped me yet. And for anyone else living with the disease, it won't stop you, either.

ACKNOWLEDGMENTS

I'd like to thank my family: my mom, Leanne; my dad, Tie; my sisters, Carlin and Avery; my aunt, Trish; my uncle, Ori; my cousins, Devan, Audrey, and Marlow; my grandma Mayrem; my grandma Connie; my grandpa Harold; all of my Coker aunts, uncles, and cousins.

Thank you to my friends: Robert Adamo, Victor Adamo, Charlie Graham, Angelo Nitsopoulos, Rory Bell, Del Cherry.

I'd like to thank Allen Fleishman and his family; Nelson Peltz and his family; Rocket; Scott McKay; John and Lynne Doyle; Mario Boscarino; Jan Winhall; Gail, Scott, and Noah Tooke; Dr. Johanna Carlo; Maria Pereira.

Thanks to all of my doctors and nurses: Dr. Pearlman, Ana Artiles, Anita Lewis, Dr. Bruce Perkins, Dr. Mike Riddell, Dr. Anne Peters, Dr. Peter Strachan, Dr. Anthony Mascia, Dr. Tony Galea, Dr. Randy Katz.

Thank you to my chefs: Matt Binkley, Johnny Deflieze, Whitney Deflieze, Ian Ray, Emileigh Kozdas.

Thank you to Mark Lindsay and Kate Pace Lindsay, Tony Scott, Mark Scappaticci, Tony Galea, Bill Dark, Bill Comrie and family, Jeff Soffer and family, Bob Kaiser and family, Heather McDonough Domi, Mitch Goldhar, Mark Silver and family, Ted Nikolaou and family, Mark Wiseman and family, Mark Wahlberg and family, Nate Schoenfeld and family.

ACKNOWLEDGMENTS

Thanks to all of my trainers and coaches over the years: Matt Nichol, Andy O'Brien, Adam Lloyd, Mark McKoy, Charlie Francis, Darryl Devonish, Jorge Blanco, Lisa and Rachel Schklar, Lawson Hammer, Dave Reid, Ben Velasquez, Tony Scott, Ian Macintyre, Vic Vescio, Mike Carneiro, Petey Asaro, Jan Winhall, Tommy Powers, Adam Oates, Dawn Braid, Ryan Barnes, Tracey Wilson, Troy Smith, and the EXOS team in Scottsdale, Arizona.

Thanks to all my teachers and classmates at Upper Canada College, St. Michael's College, and Saunders Secondary School.

Thank you to the hockey players that I looked up to and gave me motivation as a kid to play in the NHL: Bobby Clarke, Mats Sundin, Patrick Kane, Sidney Crosby, Mario Lemieux, Wayne Gretzky, Mark Messier.

Thanks to all of the London Knights staff: Dale Hunter, Mark Hunter, Dylan Hunter, Doug Stacey, Andy Scott, Chris Maton, Kim Sutherland, Jeff Paul, Rob Simpson, Rick Steadman, Rob Ramage, Natalie Wakabayashi, Geoff Haire, Dr. Dieter Bruckschwaiger, Misha Donskov.

Thanks to all of the Hockey Canada staff: Scott Salmond, Benoit Groulx, Dave Lowry, Scott Walker, Bayne Pettinger, Dr. Ian Auld, Kent Kobelka, Bill Peters, Dave Cameron, Mike Yeo.

Thank you to the Arizona Coyotes organization: Olivia Matos, Dave Griffiths, JP Major, Curt Truhe, Jason Serbus, Mike Ermatinger, Mikey Griebel, Mike Booey, Don Fuller, Tommy Powers, John MacLean, Scott Allen, Rick Tocchet, Dave Tippett, Jim Playfair, Newell Brown, John Slaney, John Elkin, Dave Zenobi, Tony Silva, Jason Rudee, Eric Ford, Dr. Rob Luberto, Stan Wilson, Denver Wilson, Corey Schwab, Steve Peters, John Chayka, Steve Sullivan, Jason Rudee, Rich Nairn, Greg Dillard.

Thank you to the Montreal Canadiens organization: Marc

Bergevin, Claude Julien, Luke Richardson, Dom Ducharme, Kirk Muller, Mario Leblanc, Stephane Waite, Claudine Crépin, Alain Gagnon, Pierre Gervais, Pierre Ouellette, Pat Langlois, Rich Généreux, Graham Rynbend, Donald Balmforth, Matthew Romano, Claude Thériault, Patrick Delisle-Houde, Pierre Allard, Dr. David Scott, Dominick Saillant, François Marchand, Dr. David Mulder.

Thank you to the whole staff and all of the sponsors at JDRF, in particular Jessica Diniz. And the entire team at Dexcom.

Thank you to the staff at Ascensia Diabetes Care, especially Sandra Dallan.

Thanks to Matt Maccarone, Keesha Davis, and everyone at Nike. Thanks to everyone at Warrior, especially Jared Q, Peter Miller, and Dan Mecrones. And the entire Bauer hockey team, especially Mary Kay Messier and Justin B.

Thank you to my agent, Pat Brisson, and everyone else at CAA.

Thanks to everyone at Simon & Schuster Canada, especially my editor, Brendan May.

Thank you all of the hockey fans out there. Playing the game wouldn't be the same without you.

I'd like to thank all of the teammates who I've played with since my diabetes diagnosis:

Seth Griffith, Alex Broadhurst, Olli Määttä, Nikita Zadorov, Tyler Ferry, Scott Harrington, Tommy Hughes, Kevin Raine, Corey Pawley, Justin Sefton, Adam Restoule, Ryan Hamelin, Chris Maton, Jack Nevins, Matt Fuller, Kevin Bailie, Jared Knight, Greg McKegg, Andreas Athanasiou, Austin Watson, Dane Fox, Jarred Tinordi, Colin Martin, Brett Cook, Troy Donnay, Michael Houser, Chase

ACKNOWLEDGMENTS

Hatcher, Jake Worrad, Noah Schwartz, Tyson Teichmann, Kyle Flemington, Connor Brown, Daniel Campini, Patrick McCarron, Eric Comrie, Zach Fucale, Madison Bowey, Dillon Heatherington, Joe Hicketts, Sam Morin, Josh Morrissey, Darnell Nurse, Shea Theodore, Robby Fabbri, Frédérik Gauthier, Curtis Lazar, Connor McDavid, Nick Paul, Nic Petan, Brayden Point, Sam Reinhart, Nick Ritchie, Jake Virtanen, Kayle Doetzel, Ryan Kujawinski, Jérémy Grégoire, Yan-Pavel Laplante, Chris Bigras, Nathan MacKinnon, Morgan Klimchuk, Adam Bateman, Alex Yuill, Jordan Subban, Steve Varga, Michael Vlajkov, Bryson Cianfrone, Tomáš Tatar, Jonathan Drouin, Phillip Danault, Jeff Petry, Brendan Gallagher, Andrew Shaw, Shea Weber, Paul Byron, Jesperi Kotkaniemi, Artturi Lehkonen, Joel Armia, Jordie Benn, Brett Kulak, Victor Mete, Mike Reilly, Jordan Weal, Kenny Agostino, Matthew Peca, Nate Thompson, Charles Hudon, Nicolas Deslauriers, Noah Juulsen, Michael Chaput, Christian Folin, Ryan Poehling, Xavier Ouellet, David Schlemko, Tomáš Plekanec, Karl Alzner, Antti Niemi, Carey Price, Charlie Lindgren, Dale Weise, Clayton Keller, Derek Stepan, Oliver Ekman-Larsson, Christian Dvorak, Alex Goligoski, Christian Fischer, Brendan Perlini, Kevin Connauton, Jason Demers, Nick Cousins, Richard Pánik, Tobias Rieder, Anthony Duclair, Jordan Martinook, Brad Richardson, Jakob Chychrun, Josh Archibald, Dylan Strome, Niklas Hjalmarsson, Zac Rinaldo, Luke Schenn, Mario Kempe, Trevor Murphy, Adam Clendening, Lawson Crouse, Marek Langhamer, Nick Merkley, Kyle Capobianco, Laurent Dauphin, Adin Hill, Joel Hanley, Louis Domingue, Freddie Hamilton, Dakota Mermis, Darcy Kuemper, Scott Wedgewood, Antti Raanta, Shane Doan, Martin Hanzal, Jamie McGinn, Connor Murphy, Alexander Burmistrov, Tony DeAngelo, Ryan White, Peter Holland, Josh Jooris, Michael Stone,

ACKNOWLEDGMENTS

Teemu Pulkkinen, Tyler Gaudet, Zbynek Michalek, Jamie McBain, Justin Peters, Mike Smith, Mikkel Bødker, Antoine Vermette, Alex Tanguay, Kyle Chipchura, Klas Dahlbeck, Nicklas Grossmann, Steve Downie, Viktor Tikhonov, Stefan Elliott, Boyd Gordon, Dustin Jeffrey, Jiří Sekáč, Craig Cunningham, John Scott, Sergei Plotnikov, Anders Lindbäck, Eric Selleck, Joe Vitale, Christian Thomas, Niklas Treutle, Philip Samuelsson, Alex Grant, Mitch Marner, Matt Rupert, Julius Bergman, Michael McCarron, Aaron Berisha, Chandler Yakimowicz, Aiden Jamieson, Owen MacDonald, Josh Sterk, Chris Martenet, Brandon Crawley, Zach Grzelewski, Drake Rymsha, Jack Hidi, John Warren, Cliff Pu, Tait Seguin, Michael Giugovaz, Joel Wigle, Eric Henderson, Mitchell Kreis, Tyler Nother, Kevin Klima, Tyler Parsons, Emanuel Vella, Josh Defarias, Tristen Elie, Kelly Klima, Ryan Valentini, Chris Tierney, Bo Horvat, Ryan Rupert, Josh Anderson, Kyle Platzer, Zach Bell, Tim Bender, Santino Centorame, Miles Liberati, Remi Elie, Jacob Jammes, Anthony Stolarz, Jake Paterson, Paxton Leroux, Cam Garrow, Owen Stewart, Liam Herbst, Justin Tugwell, Spencer Hutchinson.

There isn't enough room here to thank everyone in my life who has helped me get to where I am today. I wouldn't be where I am without you. Thank you, all.

—Max Domi

In the spring of 2017 my trusty agent, Brian Wood, called me with an offer. He asked if I would be interested in meeting with Simon & Schuster about doing a book with Max Domi.

I agreed to the meeting and was fascinated with the concept. This wasn't going to be a hockey book per se. This was going to be a book about a young man who was diagnosed with type 1 diabetes when he was twelve years old and somehow beat the odds to make it to the NHL. That was all I needed to hear, and in May 2017 we started the process of putting the book together.

There are many people who made the writing of this book possible.

First off, I would like to thank my amazing wife, Patricia, and our daughters, Adriana and Cassandra. I would not have been able to write this book without their patience and understanding. Thanks to our cat KitKat (don't ask) for not erasing any of my files while she was walking across my laptop! Our dog Hershey slept through the whole thing.

As always, thanks to my parents for instilling in me the work ethic I needed to complete this task and meet all of the deadlines.

Just as the Oilers would never trade Connor McDavid, I would never trade my agent, Brian Wood, for anything. He works so hard, and if I ever need anything, he is always there for me. That's what I call an All-Star; thanks, Brian.

The staff at Simon & Schuster Canada always set the bar very high. From the publisher Kevin Hanson on down to the newest intern, you will be hard-pressed to find a finer group of people in the publishing business.

Once again, my editor, Brendan May, was awesome throughout the entire process. Brendan is as good as it gets, and he proved it helping to put this book together.

Big thumbs-up to the management and staff at my radio station, 105.9 The Region, for being so accommodating during the writing process.

A number of websites were crucial to telling Max's story. They include: jdrf.ca (juvenile diabetes), diabetes.ca, NHL.com

/Coyotes, NHL.com, TSN.ca, Sportsnet.ca, thehockeynews.com, londonknights.com, ontariohockeyleague.com, Hockeydb.com, Hockey-reference.com, Hockeyfights.com, and YouTube.com.

The Arizona Coyotes were incredibly supportive and helpful from day one. Special thanks to general manager John Chayka, Coach Rick Tocchet, executive VP of communications and broadcasting Rich Nairn, and his entire staff of dedicated professionals. Thanks to Clayton Keller, the rest of the players, and the entire Coyotes support staff.

There is a long list of Max's friends and family who all took time to speak to me. I must say that, despite their busy schedules, not one of them—including Darnell Nurse, Bo Horvat, Scott Harrington, Connor Murphy, Chris Tierney, and Josh Anderson—hesitated when I told them I needed to speak to them about Max.

London Knights trainer Doug Stacey and everyone else on the team were very generous with their time.

After speaking with Max's billet mom, Gail Tooke, I can see why Max liked her as much as he did.

Thanks to Max's personal chef in Scottsdale, Ian, for the great food and the great information. (Great tattoos, by the way. I'm due for another one.)

Not only is the Coyotes' home rink, the Gila River Arena, a solid barn to see a game, In-N-Out Burger is perfectly situated halfway between the rink and Scottsdale. (#Heaven)

Max often talks about how close he is to his sisters, Carlin and Avery, and how much they mean to him. After getting to know them better while writing this book, I can see why he thinks so highly of them.

A big stick tap to someone whom I have had the privilege of getting to know quite well over the past few years: Max's father, Tie. You might have heard of him.

ACKNOWLEDGMENTS

The glue that held this book together is the same glue that holds Max's family together: his mom, Leanne. Leanne was an invaluable resource for dates, names, and family memories.

And last, but certainly not least, there is Max Domi.

I first met Max while he was playing for the London Knights. I was cowriting his father's book at the time, and I was immediately impressed by what a mature young man Max was.

I knew Max had type 1 diabetes and that he had overcome a lot to get to where he was. But until I started working with him on a regular basis, I had no idea just how much he had to endure in order to make it to the NHL.

From May 2017 until Max left for training camp at the end of August, I would arrive at his house in Toronto once a week. I witnessed firsthand just how dedicated Max is when it comes to getting ready to play in the NHL—the blood tests, the self-injections of insulin, and everything else that goes with living life as a person with type 1 diabetes. I was even more impressed by his strict gluten-free diet and the lengths that he goes to in order to make sure he is eating the right foods. (Although I must say, gluten-free donuts do *not* taste the same as regular donuts.)

I thoroughly enjoyed getting to know Max and spending all that time together to really understand what he is all about. If I were an NHL general manager or a coach, I would say that Max Domi is the kind of quality young man who could play for my team anytime.

Thanks for a great experience, Max; and your dog Orion really is awesome.

—*Jim Lang*